PRAISE FOR
THE SEARCH FOR RESILIENCE

I've had the honour of reading *The Search for Resilience* not once, but twice – and each time, it's shifted something deep within me. This isn't just another self-development book; it's the raw and powerful story of a remarkable human who's faced immense challenges, from fertility struggles to building a multi-seven-figure empire. Sonja's journey is equal parts inspiring and life-changing. Every page is packed with lessons that will push you to take action – in your life, your mindset, and your business. This book will move you, motivate you, and most importantly, show you how to build the kind of resilience we all need. If you've ever doubted yourself or faced tough times (and who hasn't?) *The Search for Resilience* is the book you need.

– **Heidi Anderson**
PR Coach, Publicist, and Radio Broadcaster

Reading this book made me feel human and that I'm not alone. Everyone has a story, but very rarely in this day and age you see this level of authenticity. This book made me reflect back on my past and relate. It also offered me a choice: we can stay victims, daydream for a better tomorrow, freak out and try to control everything around us, or become chief and commander – or in this case *the warrior*. Sonja fails forward. She always has and she always will, and that is why she's accomplished what most believe is unimaginable. Sonja is not only providing all the insight, experience, and foresight into her story but giving every reader practical, tangible processes and systems to allow everyone to follow through on their dreams by failing forward and being okay. Simply amazing! I'm so proud of the investment you've made into yourself, taking life on by making yourself accountable and responsible for all your decisions that are based on values and driven with purpose. It is inspiring.

– Michael Daisley
Leadership Coach

Sonja's book is an absolute masterpiece, capturing the raw, beautiful and challenging journey of fertility, business, and the dance of mum life. Having walked this path alongside her, I've witnessed firsthand her incredible strength, resilience, and determination. This book is a true reflection of the warrior she is. Sonja has transformed one of the hardest chapters of her life into a source of inspiration and guidance for so many. She always believed that her difficult journey had a purpose – to make an impact and help others – and that is exactly what she's achieved. Her ability to juggle motherhood while building a thriving business, all while navigating the ups and downs of her fertility journey, is nothing short of extraordinary and deeply inspirational. This book is not just a testament to her courage but a gift to anyone facing similar struggles. Sonja is a remarkable friend, an amazing mum, and an unstoppable businesswoman. I couldn't be prouder of her for sharing her story with the world – a true leader in so many aspects of life.

– Laura Maher
Managing Director (Dear Friend)

The Search for Resilience is a deeply moving and empowering insight into personal transformation, resilience, and self-discovery. Sonja vulnerably shares her journey of navigating both personal and professional struggles to find her inner warrior. In true Sonja style, she's turned her pain into something powerful to help others. It's both relatable and actionable. This book is a timely reminder that no matter what you're facing in your personal or professional life, you can choose to awaken your inner strength and live life on your terms. It filled me with hope – Sonja is a true inspiration.

– Tahryn Bolt
Messaging and Marketing Mentor

The Search for Resilience is a raw, compelling, and profoundly honest look at what it takes to confront life's toughest challenges and emerge stronger. Yes, Sonja has been brave in the face of many challenges beyond her control, but what truly sets her apart is her courage to consciously step into hard situations, have the difficult conversations, and face the uncomfortable moments most people choose to avoid. One of the things I love most about Sonja is her unwavering commitment to personal growth and always taking radical responsibility for her happiness and success in both life and business. Her friendship, and now this book, are both the loving but firm reminders I need to call me out on my bullshit and show me where I might not be stepping up and doing the same. Sonja has an innate ability to always see the best in people, often recognising their potential before they do themselves. She's always there to give you advice that's refreshingly honest, unfiltered, and exactly what you need to hear. This is what this book is. It's the love, guidance (and much-needed pep talks!) she gives to her friends and colleagues, now shared with the world. It's a tender, loving kick up the butt and a powerful reminder that only you can take control of your life. Some parts of the book might challenge you, but they're exactly what you need to hear to make meaningful change in your life and business.

For me, this book is about more than a search for resilience – it's about searching for what truly matters and having the grit and determination to make it happen, even when it gets tough.

10/10 recommend *A Search for Resilience* for anyone seeking to take ownership of their life and grow into the person they're meant to be. It will leave you inspired, empowered, and ready to navigate your own tough seasons with courage.

– **Laura Canham**
Business and Sales Strategist (Friend)

From the moment I met Sonja, I knew she was someone extraordinary. I've watched her in awe as she's faced the most difficult and heartbreaking moments, struggling to start a family while carrying the weight of running a business, yet she has always moved forward with unwavering strength and heart. *The Search for Resilience: Awaken the Warrior in Business and Life* is not just a book; it's a soulful testament to Sonja's journey of pain, growth, healing, and rebirth. Through her raw honesty and vulnerability, she opens a space where we can all see ourselves, find comfort, and be inspired. This book offers more than just her story, it's a guide to transforming pain into power. Sonja shares practical steps for healing and building resilience, showing us that no matter the struggle, we have the strength to rise and grow.

Her words will touch your heart and remind you that, like Sonja, you too have the warrior within. This book is a gift, one that will inspire you to take bold steps, heal, and awaken your own strength. Thank you, Sonja, for sharing your soul with us all.

– Courtney Wilder
Intuitive Coach and Business Astrologer

I've had the honour of walking alongside Sonja through some of the most transformative moments in her life – from the early days of launching her business to the personal challenges of building a family. I've seen her face the heartache of miscarriages, the overwhelming pressures of scaling a business, and the delicate balance of shifting from a hands-on entrepreneur to a trusting mother. Throughout it all, Sonja has embodied resilience, compassion, and focus like few others I've known.

I was there when she first learnt to trust in the process – and I watched, amazed, as her faith and strength blossomed into a powerful story. *The Search for Resilience: Awaken the Warrior in Business and Life* is a testament to her incredible journey. She has taken a script of trauma, pain, and heartache, and turned it into a narrative of triumph, courage, and faith. It's a story that speaks to every woman who has ever faced the struggle of building a business while navigating the challenges of motherhood.

This book isn't just a collection of words – it's a warm embrace for anyone who has walked this difficult path. Sonja has poured her heart into every page, and it will inspire anyone who reads it to awaken the warrior within themselves.

– Mike Johnston
Coach and Friend

ABOUT THE AUTHOR

Sonja Pototzki-Raymond MSc is a CEO, Google Search expert, keynote speaker, author, and fertility advocate. Also known as Sonja The Search Queen, her mission is to help her clients outrank their competitors on Google.

A force to be reckoned with, in 2018, Sonja founded The Search Republic and, within 5 years, generated over $700 million in sales for her clients. With a global footprint and an active client waitlist, The Search Republic is now one of Australia's most in-demand Google-accredited digital agencies.

Holding an honours degree and a master's in marketing, Sonja combines her Google Search smarts with her big heart and passion for making a difference to her clients' bottom line, the environment, and the business community.

With over 2 decades of global marketing and advertising experience, working for many high-profile international brands including Guinness, Jameson, Nestlé, L'Oréal, Special K, and Benefit Cosmetics, Sonja is renowned for accelerating growth

and transforming businesses using ethical, effective, and sustainable Google Search strategies.

After a gruelling fertility journey put her resilience to the test, she became an outspoken fertility advocate, shining a light on what some consider a taboo subject. Through her book, *The Search for Resilience*, she aims to empower others to awaken their inner warriors, face their biggest challenges head-on, and live their dream lives.

Sonja is a loving wife to husband Kevin and a proud (and oh-so grateful) mum to daughters Saige and Willow, proving that you can have everything you want in life *if* you're willing to fight for it.

sonjathesearchqueen.com

@sonjathesearchqueen

Sonja The Search Queen

Podcast: Diary of The Search Queen

THE SEARCH FOR RESILIENCE

THE SEARCH FOR RESILIENCE

Awaken the
WARRIOR
in Business
and Life

SONJA POTOTZKI-RAYMOND

First published in 2025 by Dean Publishing
PO Box 119
Mt. Macedon, Victoria, 3441
Australia
deanpublishing.com

Copyright © Sonja Pototzki-Raymond

All rights reserved. No part of this publication may be reproduced, stored in a retrieval system or transmitted in any way or by any means, electronic, mechanical, photocopying, recording or otherwise, without the prior written permission of the publisher.

Cataloguing-in-Publication Data
National Library of Australia
Title: The Search For Resilience
ISBN: 978-1-925452-96-9
Category: Personal growth/Business

The views and opinions expressed in this book are those of the author and do not necessarily reflect the official policy or position of any other agency, publisher, organisation, employer or company. Assumptions made in the analysis are not reflective of the position of any entity other than the author(s) – and, these views are always subject to change, revision, and rethinking at any time.

The author, publisher or organisations are not to be held responsible for misuse, reuse, recycled and cited and/or uncited copies of content within this book by others.

This book contains alternative holistic treatments and details the author's use of psychedelics. The author is only detailing her unique experience and not advocating for others to use them. No part of this book is intended as a substitute for the medical advice of physicians or fertility specialists. The reader should regularly consult their own physician and experts in matters relating to their health, particularly with respect to any fertility issues or medical symptoms that may require diagnosis or medical attention. You are responsible for your health and your choices.

The author has recreated experiences from her memory and in some instances, names and identifying details have been changed to protect the privacy of individuals.

DEDICATION

To my precious children, Saige and Willow,
This book is my heartfelt gift to you, born from the deepest love and the hardest fight your dad and I have ever faced. Through every tear, every moment of doubt, and every ounce of hope we clung to, we fought with everything we had to bring you into this world. In the toughest part of our fertility journey, I made a promise – a promise that if I were ever blessed to become your mum, I would write a book and share our struggles openly, so you would know how deeply you were wanted and how fiercely we fought for you. My beautiful girls, this book is for you, with all my love.

To my incredible husband,
Thank you for your unwavering support and for always believing in me, even when I doubted myself. You have been my greatest champion, always reminding me that I can be, do, and achieve anything I set my mind to. No matter how tough the challenges we've faced, you've stood by my side, with your love and strength holding us together.
Thank you for being my safe haven, the one place where I can always find comfort, love, and peace. We've weathered some of life's hardest moments, and there is no one else I'd want to share this journey with but you. I love you more than words could ever express.

To my incredible mum, Joan,
Thank you for your extraordinary resilience and for being the greatest role model of female empowerment I've ever had the honour of witnessing. You've shown me what it means to be strong, kind, and determined, and because of you, I am everything I am in life. I love you with all my heart and am endlessly grateful for the example you've set.

To my amazing sisters – aka my besties for life,
Diana, thank you for being such an incredible role model and for setting a standard that inspires us to strive for greatness. Your love, support, and guidance have meant everything to me. I love you deeply and am so grateful for the example you've been in my life.
Linda, thank you for always bringing light, laughter, and joy into our lives. Your humour and warmth have made our family so special, and your love and kindness mean the world to me. I'm so proud of you and love you more than words can say.

CONTENTS

INTRODUCTION ~ 1
Awaken the Warrior and Live Life on Your Terms

CHAPTER 1 ~ 15
Recognise Harmful Patterns – and Shatter Them

CHAPTER 2 ~ 49
Stop Pointing Fingers and Take Ownership

CHAPTER 3 ~ 63
Get Comfortable with Uncertainty

CHAPTER 4 ~ 81
Identify the Lessons in Past Struggles – There's a Positive in Everything

CHAPTER 5 ~ 107
Master Your Mental Dialogue

CHAPTER 6 ~ 133
Reconcile with Your Inner Child

CHAPTER 7 ~ 151
Set Impenetrable Boundaries

CHAPTER 8 ~ 179
Show Up and Surrender to the Experience

CHAPTER 9 ~ 211
Vanquish Senseless Fear and Anxiety

CHAPTER 10 ~ 243
Know That Love Is the Key to Everything

BONUS SECTION ~ 283
Coming Home to Self

Acknowledgements ~ 287
Testimonials ~ 294
Endnotes ~ 300

An awakened warrior is your destiny.

AWAKENING THE WARRIOR

AWAKEN THE WARRIOR AND LIVE LIFE ON YOUR TERMS

On 27 December 2022 (my birthday), it was a sweltering and humid day in Bali. We were on our first family holiday. Sitting beside the pool in my coral bikini, I couldn't help but bask in the moment. It was a moment we had earned. It was a moment several years in the making. It was a moment that almost never came to be.

As I watched my husband playing in the pool with our beautiful baby daughter Saige, who was wearing the cutest pink and blue unicorn swimsuit and matching hat, my heart melted. I couldn't wipe the smile off my face, nor did I want to. I had earned that smile. I had earned my happiness. I had fought for it with a level of courage and resilience I never knew I had. Often, we don't really know what we're capable of until we're tested. Until we've been pushed beyond what we thought were our limits. Only by awakening the warrior within and fighting for what we want in life can we achieve our wildest dreams. I know it because I've lived it, and soon you'll know it too.

Playing together in the pool, Daddy and Saige were having the most wonderful time. Saige was fixated on the slap of her hands on the water and the resulting splashes on her face. To her, the world was new and wonderful. We can learn a lot by watching children interact with the world. Daddy was totally engrossed by Saige and how fascinated she was with the water. As I watched them play, gratitude welled up inside me. *I'm so glad we never gave up. I'm so grateful we pushed through the toughest times to arrive at this moment. If we'd given up, Saige wouldn't be here, and this moment wouldn't exist.* In that moment, I was just so... so grateful.

Finally, our life felt complete. Saige was by far the greatest gift we could have ever received. For the first time in my life, I felt like I had everything I needed. Pure bliss! The long and arduous journey to arrive at that moment was well worth the struggle, the pain, the blood, the sweat, the tears, and the torment. In fact, it couldn't have happened any other way.

We were so grateful to be parents that we were willing to go through the entire gruelling process again. We knew we had more love to give, and our beautiful amazing daughter Willow soon became the recipient of that love. If we thought our life was complete before, now we had taken it to a whole new level. She was more than worth the effort.

Although I'm so grateful to be blessed with life's greatest treasures; it certainly didn't come wrapped in a bow and handed to me. Life tested me to my limits, it made me reach into the depths of my soul and claim it. In many ways, it led me on a mighty and gruelling inner search, and that search revealed something transformative, more than I could have bargained for – *resilience*.

Research about human resilience in *American Psychologist* states that "loss or potential trauma is more common than is often believed, and that there are multiple and sometimes unexpected pathways to resilience."[1]

And for me, that was the case – the pathways to resilience revealed themselves to me in multiple and unexpected ways. But it's only in looking back that I can see that the sequence of events and the serendipitous moments all conspired for a reason. They were to create me, not break me. And I believe that is the same for you too. You're not broken. This journey called life, as cruel as it seems, is shaping your strength. And within the moments of despair, you're planting the seeds of resilience.

THE DANCE OF THE WARRIOR

None of the best things in my life came easily. I had to fight for them every step of the way. See, I'm not a lucky person. Throughout my life, I've had to make my own luck. Like most people, I've made some good decisions; I've made some bad decisions, and I've made some that were downright catastrophic. It's all a part of the dance of life. We're all doing the dance. The problem is that many of us don't know the steps, so we try to learn them on the fly. Really, we could have benefited from a good teacher. Some of us never truly master the dance. Some of us let our inner warriors sleep while life passes us by. Don't be one of those people.

Has anyone ever told you that you *can't* have it all? I'm calling BS on that right now. For years, I believed it. I didn't think I could be a successful business owner, an amazing wife, and a great mum all at once. Guess what? I could. And you can too. Anyone can. But don't expect the universe to simply hand you everything you want. It doesn't work like that. Nope, the universe doesn't do handouts.

> Whatever you want in life, you'll have to work
> for it. You may have to fight for it. You've
> got to go and get it. Claim it for yourself.

And that's why I believe in cultivating resilience and honing your warrior mindset and skills. Life is tough, and it won't grant you your wishes without some kind of sacrifice and effort. Throughout ancient history, warriors were decorated for their courage and skilful combat, but in today's world that meaning has evolved to include those who fight in an honourable way for a cause, ideal, or principle.[2]

So, what does it mean to be a warrior in life and business? A warrior isn't only about being fierce in the face of adversity. It's about knowing when to fight and when to love. It's about approaching each challenge with open-hearted bravery. Sometimes courage is moving towards something. Other times it's walking away. Sometimes it's fighting for what's right. Other times it's admitting you're wrong. Sometimes it's pushing forward with relentless determination. Other times it's surrendering to the will of the universe.

> Essentially, an awakened warrior is aware
> of how to live and act in each moment.

She knows the dance of life, and she performs it deftly. That doesn't mean she doesn't get some of the steps wrong from time to time. None of us are perfect after all. But she persists and she faces life with humility and honour. As said in *Mulan*, "The flower that blooms in adversity is the rarest and most beautiful of all."

Dancing with life's battles blossoms the warrior within. These challenges arrive in our personal lives and in our professional lives, for the two coexist. You take yourself everywhere you go, so what happens in your personal life can affect how you show up in your professional life, and vice versa. And that's why this book blends both aspects – for awakening the warrior in business and life is both the journey that I took, and also the promise that I give to readers. You can – and most certainly will – transform your life and mindset if you participate in the activities and delve deep into self-reflection. You will become the warrior you were born to be.

From a young age, dance has been a big part of my life. I always used it as a way to express myself, cultivate training and discipline, and allow my body to fuse movement and emotion.

Dance is woven into the fabric of our humanity and nature. For thousands of years, dance has been an important aspect of many warrior cultures. It's rarely just about the dance steps; it's about the mindset, the preparation, the symbology and meaning. Warriors dance to align their minds, bodies and spirits. They dance to create a fusion with their spiritual destiny while remaining fully human in their earthly duties. It's an ancestral link between the unseen and the seen, between the physical and the spiritual.

It's also about controlled movement, sensory awareness, and synchronising with something greater, an embodied wisdom that somehow knows and senses things beyond our mortal minds. The dance of the warrior acts as a deeper connection to others and the environment, and our souls. It not only changes the way we feel but also the way we think and act.[3]

We must learn to own our unique warriorship and dance with the variables of life, keeping ourselves in rhythm to our greater destiny while doing the practical steps. Life isn't going to hand you your dreams on a silver platter; it's up to you to find them and grab them.

When I started my business, I was full of fear, self-doubt, and anxiety. Imposter syndrome to the max. Sound familiar? But with each small step, each fear faced, each adversity overcome, I grew stronger, more resilient. At a certain point, I thought I could handle anything the world threw at me. I was unstoppable. Then my husband and I faced a 3-year-long fertility journey – a fertility fight – that almost broke me. As it turned out, I still had a lot more growing to do. Even now, I'm still a work in progress. And here's the thing: the work *never* stops. But it's during the battles we face where we really discover our edge.

> And often, the hardest battle you will
> ever have to fight is the one within,
> the one between who you are now and
> who you want to be in the future.

During my toughest times, through trial, error, more trial, and much more error – I can't overstate how many times I messed up along the way – I learnt the most critical moves of the dance of life. I learnt that the process was the journey and every step along the way has a place and a purpose. Sometimes our aim is to express joy and celebrate. Other times it is to heal. Sometimes, like the ancient warrior, we strategise our moves and gain energy from Source. As you learn the dance of life, you will get some steps wrong – you may even fall on your arse – but it's all part of the art of mastery, of cultivating a warrior's grace and mindset.

This journey, however, doesn't come without battle scars – you certainly will obtain some, but those seared with scars often gain the deepest understanding and most transformative results.

> *"A warrior is not defined by her battle scars but by the strength with which she rises after each fall."*
> – Unknown

A Warrior Unearthed

Life is destined to have obstacles; no one makes it without their fair share of hurt, grief, and challenges; it's inevitable, and no one is immune. Without a strong mental attitude and philosophy characterised by resilience, love, and focus, it can be almost unbearable for some.

A true warrior in business and life doesn't aim to become hardened by life's brutal moments, but instead, a warrior becomes stronger, deeper, and wiser because of them. It is the mindset that develops the character and uses the hardships to cultivate a sense of purpose and meaning. While warriorship is often associated with soldiers, athletes, and martial artists, it is really a mindset and way of being that anyone can apply. For me, my business, my fertility journey, my personal growth, and my relationships have all been teachers that enabled me to find my deepest truth and align myself with my values, mission, and meaning. This is the true journey, who we *become* as we adventure through life.

Looking back, I needed to experience each and every one of my triumphs and failures because they became my biggest lessons. As spiritual teacher Caroline Myss points out, "Life is a journey of either Fate or Destiny. Fate is the result of giving in to one's wounds and heartaches. Your Destiny unfolds when you rise above the challenges of your life and use them as Divine opportunities to move forward to unlock your higher potential."

I learnt that in order to break the harmful patterns in our lives – that is, harmful habits, behaviours, situations that keep repeating – we must first learn to recognise them. It may sound like a no-brainer, but so many people – my former self included – go through life not knowing why the same problems keep appearing again and again and again. They don't see the patterns.

Recognising and shattering the harmful patterns in your

life is the first dance move you'll learn in this book. Oh, but we're just getting warmed up.

For years, I blamed other people – my parents, friends, colleagues, whoever I could point a finger at – for my problems. I never took ownership and acknowledged my part in everything that was wrong in my life. You have much more control over your life than you might think, and blaming others for your problems means you'll never solve them – because the responsibility lies with you. **No longer pointing fingers and instead taking ownership of your problems** is the second powerful dance move you'll learn.

Through trials and tribulations, one also gets faced with one of life's ultimate truths: that life is unpredictable and wild. That no matter how organised you are, no matter how smart and strong you are, life will dish out its fair share of uncertainty. It's uncharted territory, and there's only one compass – your soul. **Learning to embrace uncertainty and flow** is the third dance move you'll learn.

When the same problems continue to show up in your life, it usually means you're not getting the lesson you were meant to learn. Been there. Many times. Story of my life. Each misstep, failure, and undesirable outcome is an opportunity to learn and grow, but you must be willing to accept the lesson. **Identifying and accepting the lessons in past struggles** is the fourth awesome dance move you'll learn.

As you work towards your goals, your inner dialogue can either support or sabotage you. What's yours doing right now? Does the little voice in your head talk to you like a dear friend? Or is it more like a bitter enemy? Due to self-esteem issues, I wrestled with my mental dialogue for years before I finally managed to tame it. Now, I'm my own best friend, and that little voice offers nothing but support… most of the time. Hey, we all have our bad days. **Mastering your mental dialogue** is the fifth dance move you'll learn.

Part of mastering my mental dialogue and becoming my own best friend involved healing past trauma. As it turned out, many of my issues in adult life stemmed from my childhood. Do you have any unresolved issues from your childhood that are negatively impacting your adult life? If so, you're far from alone. **Reconciling with your inner child** is the sixth dance move you'll learn.

For most of my life, I was terrible at setting boundaries. I wanted everyone to like me, so I let them walk all over me. Common story, I know, which is why **setting impenetrable boundaries** is the seventh dance move you'll learn. By now, the dance will really be coming together.

During our fertility journey, I fought so hard to become a mum. I did everything in my power to make it happen, but that didn't mean it *would* happen. At a certain point, I realised I had to sit back and accept the outcome the universe provided. **Showing up and surrendering to the universe** is the eighth powerful dance move you'll learn. It's one that comes easy to some and not so easy to others. If you're a control freak like me, the idea of surrendering can be scary.

How many of your decisions come from a place of fear? How many come from a place of love? Difficult to answer, I know. So many of us are ruled by fear, but it doesn't serve us. It only holds us back from our goals and reaching our full potential. Is fear stopping you from realising your dreams? If so, it won't for much longer. **Vanquishing senseless fear and anxiety** is the ninth dance move you'll learn. It's a doozy, I know, but you'll be amazed at what you can accomplish when fear isn't a factor.

Finally, the tenth and final dance move is **knowing that love is the key to everything**. It's one thing to say it, but another to truly know and accept it. For some of us, especially those of us who've looked for love in all the wrong places – yep, that's me – it's a tough one to learn, but it's also one of the most important. It ties everything else together. To live your best possible life, all your decisions must come from a place of love, love for yourself and for others. When a warrior fights with love in her heart, she knows she's fighting for the right reasons. Love really is the key to everything.

The Search for Resilience is about more than our fertility journey. It's about the lessons I've learnt, the person I've become in the face of adversity, and the resilience I've built over time. It's a guidebook for you on your own journey through life, wherever it may take you. It's about accepting the lesson in each setback so you can keep moving forward. It's about doing the inner work, listening to your heart, and living with unrestrained authenticity. It's a call to arms for the warrior within, who's ready to awaken and make her mark on the world.

A warrior knows when to dance, when to fight, and when to sit in silence. Like the willow tree, she bends to the wind when necessary, but she doesn't let it knock her down. Through struggle, she grows stronger, more resilient. You are that warrior. You are that resilient willow. If you don't already know it, by the end of this book, you will. It's time to awaken the warrior and start living life on your terms.

Note: *Throughout this book, I've included activities to help you reflect and start taking positive action in your life. Don't skip the activities. If you're not willing to do the work, you won't get the results. It's as simple as that.*

A warrior isn't all
about being fierce in
the face of adversity.
It's about knowing
when to fight and
when to love.

AWAKENING THE WARRIOR

1

RECOGNISE HARMFUL PATTERNS – AND SHATTER THEM

NOT RUNNING AWAY, BUT RUNNING TOWARDS

Moving away from my home town of Tralee, County Kerry in Ireland to attend university in Limerick when I was 18 was one of the best decisions I ever made. If I had stayed in that town, well, I saw the paths many others went down. I saw the same familiar patterns in the people around me. Those patterns often involved drugs and sometimes suicide. It's a common theme in small towns. People often struggle with their mental health, finding unhealthy ways to cope. Now, I don't mean to throw my home town under the bus, but I sincerely believe that leaving was the best move I could have made.

My dad left and moved back to Germany when I was 7 years old. This resulted in a lot of abandonment issues I had to work through in later life. Suddenly, we were a one-parent family, with mum as the sole income earner, and money was tight. In many ways, this created a type of self-reliance that shaped who I am today. But, despite my self-reliant nature, the abandonment issues would still arise. Connecting the dots backwards, it's easy to see, but it wasn't necessarily clear at the time.

In many cases, abandonment issues arise from a type of trauma or loss of a child's primary attachment. This wound leads to deep feelings of insecurity, worthlessness, and mistrust. And the young brain, which is still forming, can be affected during its fragile developmental stages, and this can result in the child forming long-lasting issues around fear of rejection, safety, and can even lead to difficulty forming healthy adult relationships later in life.[4]

This certainly happened to me, although I didn't know it at the time. Nevertheless, growing up, I often pushed my issues aside and kept my sights on bigger things.

In 2005 I moved to Limerick to better myself and my future. However, I had to work hard to finance my own education. But I was full of grit and determination to make something of myself and avoid being a grim statistic that I'd seen so many others in my age group succumb to. Ireland isn't like Australia. There are no student loans for higher education. If you want to go to university, you better be ready to fund it yourself unless you have affluent parents.

In my first year of university, I worked in Dunnes Stores supermarket deli in Limerick, serving fresh meats, hot food, and salads. Funnily enough, a guy I knew from my home town, Kevin (or as I knew him then, Pinky), ended up becoming my manager at the Dunnes Stores supermarket. It was his first managerial job; he was reserved and quiet, and I was – quite deliberately – difficult to manage. He'd ask me to do something, and a typical response from me would be, "No, Pinky. Who do you think you are? Don't be telling me what to do. You do it." In all fairness, I'd known him since I was 11 years old, and I couldn't see him as my boss, so I challenged him on everything.

When I was young, I was a freestyle and hip-hop dance champion. Mum put my sisters and me into dancing early. It was our therapy, and it kept us off the streets and out of trouble… mostly. I put everything into dancing. I wanted to be great, and eventually I was. It was the first time I really understood that I could achieve anything I put my mind to, a realisation that would serve me well all throughout my later life. In 2003, I performed on MTV, and, in 2001, I was asked to join the Irish team and also represent Ireland in Slovenia. I was on fire! Dance taught me about the intersection between art, discipline, and self-expression. It was everything I loved.

My friend Emma and I used to practise our doubles routines in her front garden. Kevin was one of several boys who would hang out and watch us perform. While he was good-looking, and there was something different about him, he wasn't the usual type I went for. Or so I thought.

DRAWN TO ANOTHER PLACE

After my first year of university, I left my job at Dunnes Stores to work at Meteor Mobile Communications selling mobile phones. I started in the Tralee Co Kerry store in 2006 and was later transferred to underperforming stores in Limerick to help boost their performance. Through this job, I won numerous awards for my sales skills. The art of selling came naturally to me, as once I'm passionate about something and if I believe it will make a difference in someone's life, I see myself as recommending, not selling, and I made a lot of commission, which allowed me to continue to finance my education. I stayed with the company for 5 years before moving on to agency land.

After 5 years of university and hard work, I earned a Bachelor of Business (honours), majoring in marketing and management from the Limerick Institute of Technology, and a Master of Science (MSc) for marketing, consumption, and society from the University of Limerick. I was proud of my achievements and ready to unleash my potential.

I went on to work in marketing, working with several well-known global brands in Ireland, including Guinness, Mazda, Jameson, Skoda, Special K, Nestlé, L'Oréal, and Heineken. I also won numerous awards for sales and was even a top country sales manager for a global cosmetics brand Benefit Cosmetics. Although I established a strong career and great reputation in Ireland, I knew I was destined for bigger and sunnier things. Australia was calling... and so was my destiny.

Why Australia? Well, it has an interesting backstory. An ex-boyfriend, Aiden, emigrated to Australia in 2004. I had fallen hard for him back in the day, and he held a deep love of Australia that had lit a fire inside me. When he spoke of this country, a little voice inside of me just knew that one day I'd move there too. It's that kind of intuitive knowing when you know it in your heart before it happens in reality. Then in 2016, Aiden tragically died in a motorbike accident. Shock swept through me. Although we were no longer together, we had a soul connection that transcended time and space.

My relationship with Aiden was a massive learning curve, and he was one of my greatest teachers. Our brief relationship taught me so much. When he left for Australia, my wounds of abandonment got ripped open and triggered again. My original 'father wound' was now added to with Aiden's sudden departure from this realm, and my soul was aching for reasons I couldn't explain. I think that's what happens sometimes when we move through rites of passage of pain and transformation. Our hearts break open, and we're faced with our raw, deep, and unconscious patterns. Although nothing can remedy it in the moment, the pain is a hidden treasure for our spiritual growth in the long term.

I had to do a lot of inner work to reconnect back to myself, as it felt like the wound of abandonment was fragmenting me and I needed to find new ways to be whole within. Aiden's spiritual self didn't leave me though; he sent signs and synchronicities to show me that he was watching over me. I realised over time that this meaningful spiritual connection was medicine to my wound; he was a part of my story and a part of my growth. His curiosity towards Australia stuck with me and, in many ways, led me to the next part of my destiny. I knew in my heart of hearts that I would one day move to Australia; it wasn't a matter of *if*, but *when*. The timing had to be right.

I knew Ireland wasn't where I was meant to stay forever; I had more harmful patterns to break first, but I longed to find my place in the world. I could feel a calling to live my fullest potential, and I would always walk towards this calling and honour its silent whispers.

Breaking Patterns

In Ireland, I was always trying to fit in, going as far as to change my personality so people would accept me. Being half German, I didn't look very Irish and didn't have an Irish surname, which made fitting in even harder. Yep, I stood out like a sore thumb.

The pattern of trying to fit in followed me through childhood and into the beginning of my career, especially when I worked in cosmetics. It was a very cliquey industry, and I couldn't figure out why I didn't fit in with the clique. Eventually, I realised it was because I refused to engage in gossip and bitch about people behind their backs. Did I really want to fit in with that? Was that *really* what I wanted to do? The thing was, the more I tried to fit in, the less I actually did fit in. Ironic, right? I was repeating the same pattern, failing to show up as my true self, and gaining nothing from it. Clearly, it was a pattern I needed to break. Recognising this was the first step. Breaking it, and avoiding slipping back into it, would take serious conscious effort.

Nowadays, I don't fit in at all, and I don't care. Why? Because I don't want to fit in. I believe that our conditioning around needing to fit in stems from the mainstream schooling system. When industrialist John D Rockefeller was 'transforming' the western schooling system, he said, "I don't want a nation of thinkers, I want a nation of workers." It's a dark truth that's often hard to face. It was all about creating a society of indoctrinated workers that fed the economy and conformed to rules. But fitting in isn't what we're meant to do, ever.

As far as I'm concerned, fitting in is something no one should ever strive to do. A warrior isn't born to fit in. A warrior is born to stand up, and even stand out if required. She carves her own path through life. She doesn't simply fall in step with the masses and tread the beaten track. She blazes the trail herself and doesn't look back. As Joan of Arc said, "I am not afraid… I was born to do this."

Even back then, I knew authenticity mattered, and I was willing to fight for the right to show up as my authentic self in every part of my life. It's a big part of why I've been so wildly successful. I now own every part of myself – the good, the badass, and the awesome.

I feel like the conditioning we receive in school makes many of us think we *need* to fit in to be successful. In mainstream schools – at least in my experience – everyone is expected to learn the same things from the same textbooks, wear the same clothes, act the same, speak the same, behave the same. "Get in line. Don't speak out of turn. Do what you're told." I believe the school system is a big part of why people are afraid to stand out. Standing out means you've stepped out of line; therefore, you must be punished. They're grooming students to service the big corporations, not inspiring them to dream big and disrupt the status quo. It's the system feeding the system, and it makes us scared to step outside of our comfort zones. For years, I felt the pressure to fit in, stay in line, follow the rules, but it wasn't me. It wasn't the authentic me. It was simply a pattern I had fallen into and repeated again and again. Do you want the good news? All patterns can be broken, and all harmful patterns *should* be broken. Are any patterns in your life holding you back? Now's the time to break them. In fact, we're gonna break them at the end of this section!

Once I decided to be the designer of my own life journey, I didn't feel the need to fit in anymore. I didn't feel the need to conform and follow the typical path, where I would only find heartbreak, misery, and other people's failures. I knew it wasn't the path for me. I knew I was meant for more. Are you walking your ideal path, or simply walking where others have already trod?

I'm a huge Disney fan, so humour me while I talk about Moana. In Moana, her father wishes for her to stay on the island, believing that life beyond the reef was too dangerous. But journeying beyond the 'danger' was the only way for Moana to save her people, so she took the risk. She did what she knew she needed to do, even if it didn't conform with what others believed. In the past, I allowed the opinions of others to impact me, which resulted in me losing trust in my intuition. Gradually, I learnt to trust my gut again, and it was telling me that my life in Ireland was coming to an end.

I saw how powerful moving away from my home town had been, and I knew another big move was in my future. However, the timing never felt right. If I went too early, before I had my shit together, I'd mess up my chance of getting a visa. I had to play it smart and not rush into anything, regardless of how sure I was of the move. My inner knowing told me Australia was the place for me. I just needed to wait for the right time to make the move.

Eventually, my sister Diana decided to emigrate to Australia for a year (15 years later, and she's still living in Perth), moving within 6 months of making the decision. It had to be a sign, right? For me, it was more of a 10-year journey from initial decision to the move, but at age 26 I finally arrived in Australia, with the mature (enough) head on my shoulders I needed to make the most of the opportunity.

INNER WARFARE: AN ACTIVITY TO AWAKEN YOUR WARRIOR

Identify Harmful Patterns in Your Life – and Shatter Them

To break unproductive patterns, you first need to know what they are. Think back over the past few weeks, months, years, decades, and identify any repeating situations, behaviours, or outcomes that aren't serving you. **Write them down.**

Now identify the actions you'll take or changes you'll make to break them. **Write them down.**

For example, one pattern I found myself repeating over and over again was letting toxic people into my inner circle. Because I wanted so badly to be liked and feel worthy, I let people treat me badly. What I realised I needed was fewer (really none) of those types of people in my life and more people who lifted me up instead of pulling me down.

So, for my **harmful pattern**, I'd write: *Letting toxic people into my life.*

How did I break it? I had to be diligent and set firm boundaries whenever the wrong types of people crossed my path. While totally avoiding toxic people is difficult, you don't need to let them get a foothold in your life and inner circle.

So, for my **action to break it**, I'd write: *Identify problem people, avoid when possible, and set firm boundaries when necessary.*

Simple, right? Now it's your turn to shatter some harmful patterns.

Harmful Pattern	Action to Break It

The final step? You might have guessed it... Start taking meaningful action to shatter those harmful patterns like the resilient warrior you are. You've got this.

NEW SHORES, NEW HOME, AND A NICE SURPRISE

I arrived in Perth on 2 October 2013 and 2 weeks later, I met up with some people from my home town. On 20 October, we went to a friend's place for a Sunday sesh, and Kevin of all people happened to be there. He had moved to Australia on the same date as me 2 years prior. Coincidence? Or the universe working in mysterious ways?

When I first saw Kevin at the house, I was taken aback by his dress sense and how handsome he was. Was this really the same guy I had known for all those years? The guy who was my manager when I worked at Dunnes? He also had a tattoo sleeve, and was looking more bad boy than ever. Something within me stood up and took notice. As fate would have it, Kevin and I literally spent the entire day talking about our life journeys and what we had both been through. He had lost his girlfriend to leukemia in 2007 when he was 24. One of my close family members was diagnosed with cancer the same year. The conversation then shifted to big-picture topics, including the meaning of life. We just talked and talked and talked and talked. There was no shutting us up. It wasn't just idle chitchat; it was soul-nourishing — no holds barred — open-hearted talking.

Eventually, we all decided to go to the Shed, a popular pub in Perth for Irish people having a Sunday sesh. In order to get in, Kevin had to change his shoes, so we went back to his place, which overlooked the Swan River. It was a beautiful apartment, and he was completely set up, which, to someone fresh off the boat, was very impressive. Clearly, he was doing quite well for himself.

On my way to the balcony, I broke my shoe. At this point, I had only been in Australia for 2 weeks, so I was staying with my sister while I got set up. Kevin wasn't drinking, so he offered to drive me home to get a new pair of shoes. While we were there, he held my 1-week-old niece Millie-Mai, and I could see that he was born to be a father. There was no doubt about it. Both gentleness and masculinity oozed from him as he cradled Millie-Mai.

When we got to the pub, Kevin and I continued to chat. We connected in a way we never had before. So much so that, out of nowhere, he went for the kiss – completely sober, no drink in him at all.

Wow! My head went into a spin. *What's happening here? Kevin's such a nice guy… but he's not usually the type I go for… but he's changed a lot. He's now kissing me. Maybe those past relationships with the typical guys I go for never worked out for a reason. Maybe it's time to break another pattern.*

FINDING CALM IN THE STORM OF MY LIFE

When I met up with Kevin in Australia, I was lost, insecure, and battling a whirlwind of demons. I couldn't seem to break the pattern of letting toxic people into my life. In the storm of my life, Kevin became my safe port.

Even so, we had our struggles. I was dealing with a lot – where do I start? – and Kevin struggled with opening up. How could I be with someone who was emotionally unavailable? We were both trying to master the dance of love, and it was clear we had some work to do on ourselves for the relationship to work.

At one point, we broke up, and I thought the relationship was over for good. The fireworks just weren't there. Besides, did I really want to move to the other side of the world to be with someone who had lived 5 minutes from where I grew up? Was that really breaking the pattern? Thankfully, my mum talked some sense into me when she was visiting us in March 2014.

"There are no fireworks between me and Kevin," I told her.

"Don't you be chasing those fireworks," she said. "You'll get burnt. It happened to me with your father. Kevin's a good guy with a good head on his shoulders. He's a fabulous human."

She was right. Kevin is like Mr Miyagi in *The Karate Kid*. He has such a calming presence. He even has a martial arts black belt. When you're in his company, you instantly feel calm and safe. He doesn't even have to say anything. He's quick to action in a crisis, often jumping in to help before anyone even knows what's happening. He was my safety net, the person I had been searching for all my life. It just took me a while to realise it.

GOING OUT WITH A BANG

The theme of breaking patterns in relationships didn't just apply to men or intimate relationships; it was also raising its ugly head in my working relationships with colleagues and bosses. But you know what happens, right? When you need to learn something, the universe offers it to you, and if you don't learn the lesson the first time, it keeps appearing. As spiritual teacher Eckhart Tolle said, "Life will give you whatever experience is most helpful for the evolution of your consciousness. How do you know this is the experience you need? Because this is the experience you are having at the moment."[5]

Little did I know it at the time, but I was about to come face-to-face with another pattern that required recognition and breaking. It was as subtle as a sledgehammer, and I was forced to take notice.

When I first arrived in Australia, I worked at a couple of different marketing agencies. At the first agency, I was forced to keep my head down and my mouth shut, even in the face of unethical behaviour. If I rocked the boat too much, I risked losing my visa and being sent back to Ireland. However, once I gained permanent residency, it was open season, and I resigned the very next day.

At the second Australian agency I worked at, I found similar patterns repeating, the same destructive patterns I had witnessed in other workplaces. To fit in, I had to be cliquey. I had to fit a certain stereotype. I had to be bitchy, gossipy, and self-serving. It was like the movie *Mean Girls*. It was that bad. But I wasn't that type of person, and it certainly wasn't someone I was willing to become.

I saw young people join the agency, and the minute they walked in the door, they were groomed and brainwashed into accepting the company culture, working 70 hours a week for a mere $40K a year. It was horrendous, but unfortunately it's something that happens a lot in the industry.

Luckily, I recognised it for what it was. Familiar patterns, remember? I refused to fall into line. I refused to keep my mouth shut. I refused to fit the mould. I had experienced enough bullying in my life, especially in school, to know I didn't want anything to do with that type of behaviour. So, I resigned. Boom!

At the third agency, I was tasked with handling one of their biggest clients. The client wasn't happy with the previous account manager. There was a personality clash, and we risked losing the client altogether. To my horror, the situation was worse than I thought.

Upon investigating the client's SEO campaign, I realised their website was being penalised by Google and they were losing potentially millions of dollars in business. How could this happen? Well, there are over 5,000 algorithm changes each year when it comes to Google search, and every business needs a good SEO strategy to adapt to those changes and stay ahead of the game. Unfortunately, the SEO campaign, which the agency had outsourced to an overseas company, was using what we call 'black hat' tactics. In short, they were trying to *trick* Google into ranking the website highly instead of playing by the rules. When you do this, it's only a matter of time before Google finds out and turns on you, potentially preventing your site from appearing in search results altogether. Yep, it's a big deal. For a business that's relying on search traffic to generate revenue, being put in Google jail can be a death sentence, which is why black hat tactics are never worth it in the long run. While 'white hat' – or 'best practices' – SEO requires time and patience, it's the safer and ultimately more effective approach. If someone offers quick short-term results when it comes to climbing the Google rankings, run for the hills. It's a massive red flag, and they'll likely say and do anything just to get a sale. To get Google's trust, you have to earn it, and there are no shortcuts, only effective long-term strategies.

Anyway, the company we outsourced to hadn't entirely taken a white hat approach, which was causing problems. I explained to my boss what had happened, but he didn't seem to grasp the severity of the situation. He didn't even know what SEO entailed. He did, however, understand that we were in danger of losing our biggest client, and he begged me not to tell them. *What?* I couldn't agree to that. It went completely against my morals. *Sonja, you can't work here any longer*, I told myself. I had to draw the line.

In the weeks that followed, as I considered my options, the situation only got worse. When I gave my recommendations for how to move forward with the client, my boss responded with, "What do you know? You're just a woman." Yep, in this day and age. *What the fuck?* Clearly, it was time to go.

Time and time again in the industry, I saw the same harmful

pattern: toxic work environments and agencies willing to use unethical tactics to get ahead. Who was to say I wouldn't be walking into a similar situation at another agency? The warrior within knew exactly what she had to do. It was time to break yet another pattern and start doing things my way. *Why shouldn't I go out on my own? My clients respect me, and I could do things better and, unlike many others, ethically. What am I waiting for?* It was time to rise above the BS in the industry and play the game by my rules, focusing on trust, respect, loyalty, and integrity (four words that are now the pillars of my business and everything we do). Really, it's what all businesses should be striving for.

In August 2018, ten previous clients I had worked with at other agencies approached me and encouraged me to start my own business. With a fire burning inside me, I left the security of employment and chose to go out on my own. I handed in my resignation and decided to take a chance – founding what would eventually become The Search Republic. It was absolutely the right decision. Within 5 years, we generated over $700 million for our clients and quickly became one of Australia's most in-demand Google-accredited digital agencies. This girl was on fire!

For your reading pleasure, I've included the email I sent to my boss right before I left. As you'll see, I didn't pull any punches. Like the ancient warrior, I chose the art of moving towards battle rather than retreating. Sometimes you have to put on your armour and head directly into unchartered territory. You have to face the dragons that want to breathe fire on you.

A Parting Email to My Employer

Hi ,

Just coming back to you regarding your request for me not to tell ████████ that I am leaving ████████.

I have spoken at length with Kevin this evening about this, I am extremely uncomfortable with this and I find it quite surprising that you are asking me to not tell them despite having worked alongside them for the last 4 months. Do you expect them to forget I ever existed and that they will forget about me, I don't think so? How you believe clients are to be managed is based on results however mine is first and foremost about respect and the relationship.

Being dishonest with clients is not something that I am prepared to do and it is certainly not how I believe anyone should do things and honesty is the reason as to why I have so many long term standing relationships with past clients, however it seems to me that this is something you and others in the office are accustomed to but this is certainly not me.

To be perfectly honest I don't feel I have any loyalty or any need to have your back on this and lie for you especially when you don't have anyone else's back bar your own and maybe one or two others in the office. Sooner or later when people continuously go out of their way to upset people it eventually comes back to bite them in the arse in which it is very clear that this is happening here as you are obviously afraid that you are going to lose ▮▮▮▮ if I tell them I am leaving due to the relationship that they have with me, I don't need to point out the obvious here ▮▮▮▮ but what does that say about you?

As discussed with you on many occasions and again on Monday I have done everything in power to help the agency and people succeed given my experience working in 4 other agencies, unfortunately, I can only help people who are open to change and it is very clear that you aren't open to it and you seem to think you can do everything better than anyone else, it's like it is a game to you. It is extremely dysfunctional in my opinion.

> *"It doesn't make sense to hire smart people and then tell them what to do; we hire smart people so they can tell us what to do."*
> – Steve Jobs

My time at ▮▮▮▮ has 100% been the worst place I have ever worked in and I know I am not the only one that feels this way, as I said to you on ▮▮▮▮, there comes a time when we have to realise that we are the common denominator as to why people are constantly leaving, I recall there has been a total of 29 people who have left in a 2 year period.

████████ is no longer a place I would like to associate myself with after the ████████ given that this is my leave date.

I can see that you are in a situation that if ████████ leaves ████████ due to my departure, this is going to impact your personal relationship with ████████ and ultimately impact the company as a whole.

Considering all the above there are 2 options on how to move forward and I will leave with you:

Option 1
- I can tell ████████ by the end of this week ████████ that I am leaving ████████ for good after the ████████.
- I was going to use ████████ as a reference for my future endeavours with prospective employers, by me not telling them that delays my search for employment.

Option 2
Considering I have always stayed true to myself and I did the right thing by handing in my notice before I left for the wedding, I could have very easily kept all my holiday pay and not returned after the wedding which you suspected was going to happen, however I would never do that as that would be intentionally going out of my way to create drama, which ultimately would only end up coming back

to bite me in the arse.

Let me remind you that the leave that I had for my wedding was already negotiated into my contract with you when I started, and this approved PAID leave was signed by you on ▓▓▓▓ please see attached. It was agreed that I would be paid this and not go into negative leave due to all the overtime I did when ▓▓▓▓ left the Company.

- If I don't tell ▓▓▓▓, then I expect that technically I would still be employed by ▓▓▓▓ until ▓▓▓▓ then essentially, I wouldn't be dishonest by not telling them.
- If you don't want me to say anything, then the following are the conditions that I want to be fulfilled:
  - ~ Pay me my 6 weeks leave that was already promised to me, however I expect this to be in one lump sum of $15k – which is for the 6 weeks that I will be away.
  - ~ The laptop is mine to keep as I need it for when I go home for the wedding to plan everything and to apply for jobs while I am away.
  - ~ I am on a work contract for my phone however it's my personal number that I migrated to ▓▓▓▓, so I want to keep my number as well as my phone.
  - ~ I expect a glorified written reference before I leave.
  - ~ Please note I would expect all funds to be paid

before ▨ otherwise I will tell ▨ on ▨.

~ That when I don't return to work after the ▨ that you don't expect me to pay back my holidays?

At the end of the day I have nothing to lose here so the ball is in your court, I am already at a loss and you left me no choice but to resign due to the toxic environment taking its toll on my health and personal life.

Let me know how you want to proceed by COB tomorrow ▨ otherwise I am telling ▨ on Friday and you can deal with the ramifications after that.

I know how the world works! Not just a pretty face ▨.

Warm Regards,
Sonja Pototzki
Head of Account Management

In case you're wondering, he chose option one.

DEFINED VALUES – THE PILLARS OF ANY SUCCESSFUL BUSINESS

My business values of trust, respect, loyalty, and integrity form the foundation of everything I do at The Search Republic.

They're not just my values; they're shared values. My team, my clients, and I are all aligned… for the most part. If I happen to misread a client and our values don't match, I fire them. It's a perk of running your own business. You *can* fire clients. Isn't it great? Life is much more pleasant when you surround yourself with people who are aligned with you and what you believe in. Have you clearly defined your values yet, your warrior ethos? If not, why not?

For inspiration and clarity, let's do a deeper dive into my business values of trust, respect, loyalty, and integrity. They aren't just 'mine' – they're a warrior ethos that can serve you and humanity.

Trust

"Earn trust, earn trust, earn trust.
Then you can worry about the rest."
– Seth Godin

Trust is the lifeblood of any relationship, whether personal or professional. Without trust, the relationship simply can't last.

Marketing isn't an industry many people associate with trustworthiness, which is why trust is the number one value in my business. Too many business owners have horror stories about working with untrustworthy agencies. After witnessing shady tactics firsthand, I decided it was time for change. I wanted to bring transparency to the industry and restore people's trust, which risked being broken beyond repair. How can a client work with an agency they don't trust? On the flip side, how can a business owner work with a client they don't trust? Trust is a two-way street, and 'trustworthy' is a label you earn, not one you can simply slap on your business and call it a day. You must work for it.

Put yourself in the client's shoes. When you invest in a new service or business, there can be uncertainty, anxiety, maybe even fear that you've made a mistake. You don't want to waste your money on something that turns out to be rubbish. If someone is pitching you something that seems too good to be true, trust your gut. Don't get sucked in. Simply turn the other way and run. If the trust isn't there, the relationship will likely end in ruin, so save yourself the trouble and heartbreak.

As a business owner, putting yourself out there authentically on social media is a great way to build trust. By the time someone asks to work with you, they already know you and what you stand for. They know whether you're the right fit or not.

Part of maintaining trust with my clients is open communication all throughout the relationship. We don't use a 'set and forget' strategy when setting up a campaign, which I've seen some agencies do. We're constantly working away in the background, adapting and optimising campaigns, and we let our clients know in layman's terms exactly what we're doing. There's no mystery, no uncertainty, no second-guessing their decision to work with us. What you see is what you get. Deliverables and expectations are clear from the outset, and transparency is maintained all throughout the relationship.

Trust is the cornerstone of everything we do. Without it, our other values wouldn't mean a thing.

Respect

> *"Trust and respect is something you earn, not something that is given."*
> – Billie Jean King

Respect, baby! Why is respect one of my company values? Simply put, I don't engage with anyone personally or professionally who doesn't show respect. Naturally, it's a two-way street. I have the utmost respect for my clients, and I expect the same in return.

So, what does respect look like from a business perspective? For starters, I respect my clients' marketing budgets as if it's my own money. I also prioritise and treat my clients' businesses as if they're my own. Simple, right?

By showing respect and expecting it in return, I'm not only respecting my clients but myself too. I'm recognising my worth and setting a healthy boundary that benefits both my physical and mental health. We all deserve to be treated with dignity and respect.

The Dalai Lama once said, "Mutual respect is the foundation

of genuine harmony." Can't argue with that. When respect is present, it fosters loyalty, collaboration, and shared success.

Loyalty

*"You don't earn loyalty in a day.
You earn loyalty day-by-day."*
– Jeffrey Gitomer

I've always held loyalty as a personal value, but it's not something others have always reflected back at me. In my industry, I've noticed a serious loyalty drought. So, when I started my own business, I wanted loyalty to be a key component of everything we did.

To me, loyalty means several things:

- **Longevity.** We don't partner with clients if we don't see the relationship going the distance. With mutual loyalty comes longevity. We're not in this for short-term gain. Results take time, and we're all about cultivating long-lasting relationships that benefit both parties.
- **Support.** I always want our clients to feel supported. If they show us loyalty and respect, we've got their back and always will. Once you've earned my loyalty, we're in this together, and I'll defend you to the death.
- **Commitment.** Loyalty isn't just about a commitment to my clients but to myself as well. I'm committed to my

clients 100 percent, but I'm also committed to myself. I spent so many years working in agencies where loyalty was in short supply. Nowadays, it's a critical component of all my relationships.

- **Retention.** Because we express loyalty and keep our current clients happy, we're not constantly chasing new ones. Our retention rate is high, as high as humanly possible, which comes down to multiple factors, one of them being mutual loyalty between us and our clients.

When signing to a big brand, it's easy to become just a number, unseen, unheard, existing solely for profit. It's a feeling I set out to banish when I created my business. By always putting our client relationships first and demonstrating fierce loyalty, I've achieved that goal. My clients mean the world to me and my team. *Their* business success is our success. We're in this together.

Integrity

"Integrity is when what you think and what you say and what you do are one."
– Naval Ravikant

When it comes to integrity, it's pretty black and white. You either speak with honesty and do the right thing, especially when no one is watching, or you don't. It's a lesson I learnt the hard way.

After years in the digital marketing industry, I realised it was commonplace for many agencies to overpromise and underdeliver (or worse). Because many clients don't know how to check their campaign progress, they're left none the wiser.

When I set up The Search Republic (formerly known as The Marketing Republiq), I aimed to create a place where business owners who had been burnt before could feel like they were in safe hands. I had seen the mistakes other agencies had made, and I was determined to never repeat them.

Integrity is a guiding principle of any successful business. Through integrity, we build that all-important trust with our clients. I'd rather underpromise and overdeliver than leave someone feeling disappointed. Sure, overpromising might get a quick sale, but the relationship won't last – because you're starting it with a lie.

When you operate from a place of integrity – that is, always looking to do what's right rather than what's most profitable in the short term – no one can fault what you're doing. You can operate with a clear conscience knowing you're in the right.

From the outset of starting my business, defining my values was important. They've been my guiding compass in every decision I've made and every action I've taken. A true warrior isn't some mercenary who only attaches 'value' to money. Instead, she has a deep understanding of the diverse principles that guide her on every step of her journey. Importantly, she never compromises on those unwavering values. They are written in stone. So, have you defined your own values to help guide you through business and life? If not, what's stopping you? There's no better time than now.

> A warrior isn't born to fit in. A warrior is born to stand up, and even stand out if required. She carves her own path through life.

Recognise Harmful Patterns – and Shatter Them

1. Change your environment when necessary. Sometimes harmful patterns are the result of our environments, whether that be an uninspiring home town or a toxic work environment. Walking away from the familiar can be scary, but it's often the pathway to growth.

2. Don't conform to society's expectations to the detriment of your dreams and authentic self. Too often, we stunt our own growth and stifle our personalities to fit in with the crowd. Don't do that! Instead, embrace who you are and see where it takes you.

3. Looking for love? Make sure you look in the right places. Never in my wildest dreams did I imagine that Kevin and I would get together let alone become husband and wife. Don't repeat the pattern of looking for love in all the wrong places (like I did). The right partner might be in the place you least expect.

4. Define your values and live by them in business and in life. Without clearly defined values, you can't know what you stand for, which means others can't know either.

5. Trust, respect, loyalty, and integrity are crucial to any healthy relationship, whether it be personal or professional. While you may have different values from me, I firmly believe that trust, respect, loyalty, and integrity are the non-negotiables in any relationship.

You have the power.
No matter how stuck
or powerless you
might feel, you have
the power to change
your situation.

AWAKENING THE WARRIOR

2

STOP POINTING FINGERS AND TAKE OWNERSHIP

IDENTIFYING YOUR PART IN YOUR PROBLEMS

When life isn't going how you had hoped, who do you blame? The people around you? Your parents and your upbringing? The universe? Who does the warrior blame when a battle doesn't go her way? Sure, in the past, she might have blamed the gods, but a true modern warrior takes responsibility and understands her part in her problems.

Sometimes when I was struggling, I wanted someone or something to blame. The truth is, pointing fingers doesn't get you very far. In fact, it can distract from the real problems you need to address. If you're pointing the finger, you're simply not getting the lesson you need to learn. *Your* problems are *your* problems, no one else's, and it's up to you to fix them.

If something isn't going your way, you should reflect and try to identify your part in the problem. It can be a difficult dance step to learn, but it's crucial to your success and happiness. When people refuse to take accountability, it drives me bonkers. They get stuck in a loop of pointing the finger at others, and they keep repeating the same harmful patterns over and over – and we know how important it is to break those patterns, yeah? Sure, you can keep claiming that it's everyone else who's at fault, and it may be true to some extent, but you're not powerless in these situations. It's time to get serious with yourself, reflect honestly, and identify where *you* can make positive changes.

For instance, when I kept finding myself in work environments that didn't align with my values, I blamed the people at those companies. Were they in the wrong? Yes. Could I change them? I doubt it. Was it useful to keep putting myself in those same unpleasant situations? Nope. Once I realised my part in creating the problem – putting myself in unsuitable work environments – the solution seemed simple. *Okay*, I realised, *I'm not meant to work for someone else. I'm not compatible with that type of arrangement. I need to do my own thing.* See, I'm not saying you're the sole source of blame when things go wrong, but you absolutely have more power than you might think. The key is to understand this, frequently reflect, and exercise that power when necessary. As Tony Robbins said, "Who you spend time with is who you become! Change your life by consciously choosing to surround yourself with people with higher standards!"

It's Not All About You... But Sometimes It Is

When I first started my business, I came at it from the wrong angle. Initially, I started the business to create an environment where I could avoid toxic situations and do things the right way. The thing is, when you're providing a product or service, it's not all about you. It's more about the people you're trying to help. As soon as I realised this, my business went gangbusters and has only accelerated from there, with a long waitlist of clients waiting to work with me.

I quickly learnt that not every client is the right fit, just like I wasn't compatible with every workplace (or any workplace, it seemed). While I did say running a business isn't all about you, sometimes it is about you, and you need to make decisions for your own benefit and sanity.

One client, before I started working with her, put me on a pedestal. Her business was struggling, and she believed I could work literal magic to save it. I've learnt that when people put you on a pedestal, they can just as quickly put you in a pit when something doesn't go their way. Ideally, you want people treating you as an equal. When there's an imbalance in the relationship, it can lead to tough situations, as will soon be evident.

In offering my services to someone who put me on such a pedestal, I ignored an obvious red flag. I knew better, but I chose to ignore my gut instinct – always a big mistake – putting myself in a difficult and totally avoidable situation. Essentially, I was setting myself up for a battle I didn't have to fight. I could see the bigger picture, and my gut instinct was signalling 'no', but my heart often got the better of me, and I succumbed and agreed. Business ownership can be complex at times, and sometimes the inner battles we fight are important aspects of our consciousness that need to be seen and experienced in order to be overcome.

Firstly, I swear to God, the second my client signed the contract and the campaign went live, she turned into the ice queen. I had explained to her how Google Ads worked and how we needed to play the long game, but she was telling herself a different story. She wanted the quick magical fix that she thought I was capable of, even though I had gone to great lengths to explain the reality of the situation. With Google, it takes time and persistence to get results. Before taking on a new client, I always ensure they understand this. I scream it from the hilltops on socials. It's in the contract. It's explained again during onboarding. I leave no room for misunderstanding. When it comes to Google, there are no guarantees, which is why managing expectations is a critical part of what we do.

Unfortunately, the relationship with this client went sour almost immediately. Two months into the agreement, I accepted, in my attempt to help, I had created a stressful situation for myself, not to mention that the client didn't seem to want my type of help anyway. I decided it would be best for both of us if we went our separate ways. It was a retreat of sorts, but I knew I was fighting a losing battle. A warrior knows when to break away to live to fight another day. As I ended the arrangement, I explained to her again how the process worked and how we weren't working as a team, which is essential to success. I can't help someone if they're resisting my advice and all the necessary steps to get results. Essentially, she wanted a lottery win, not an earned outcome. She's not alone in her thinking. There are plenty of other business owners out there who want the quick fix. You can see how it might be easy for crafty salespeople to entice people with unrealistic promises. They simply tell people what they want to hear, no matter how unrealistic it might be.

By understanding I had the power to change the situation – that is, remove myself from it – I was able to fire that client and focus on people who actually wanted my help. If she had instead accepted her part in the problem – yeah, it was never going to happen – she might have received a more favourable outcome. The reality was, her business was failing, and she came to me for help. She wasn't willing to accept her part in the problem or the solution, which led to her putting her business on the line. It's a powerful lesson in taking ownership.

While I had done everything in my power to help that client understand the reality of the situation, I still had a responsibility to myself and my business. Sure, I could have continued to blame her for the difficult relationship and kept trying to win her over. But did I really want that stress in my life? No way. In the end, it was my responsibility to end the arrangement so we could both get on with our lives. Accepting your part in every unpleasant situation isn't about blaming yourself. It's about knowing you have the power to change it.

INNER WARFARE: AN ACTIVITY TO AWAKEN YOUR WARRIOR

Accept Your Part in Your Problems and Take Action

If you're in the habit of pointing the finger at others for your problems, whether it's other people, your circumstances, your upbringing, the government, the universe, whatever, it's time to take ownership. Think about it. If you believe others are to blame for your problems, it means you don't have the power to solve them yourself. Pretty bleak reality, right? Luckily, it's not true, and you absolutely do have the power.

I want you to think of some less-than-ideal situations you're currently in and struggling to overcome. **Write them down**. Next, do some serious reflection and identify your part in the problem. What actions or behaviours are facilitating or fuelling the problem? **Write them down.**

For example, in the case of the client I had to fire, the undesirable situation was having to deal with a difficult lady who didn't actually want my help or advice, at least not in the way I offered it. So, for an **undesirable situation**, I'd write: *Being stuck with a difficult client while fighting a losing battle.* The initial action that led to my predicament was taking her on as a client despite the red flags. I then continued to try to help her, even though it was clear she wasn't willing to play ball. So, for **my part**, I'd write: *Taking on a difficult client and continuing to try to help someone who clearly doesn't want the services I actually offer.*

See, once I understood my part in the problem, I could come up with a solution. No one had a gun to my head saying I had no choice but to continue working with this client. When I thought about it, I realised I had the power to change the situation, and I didn't need to keep bending over backwards for someone who wasn't willing to do her part. I could simply end the arrangement and focus on helping people who were actually receptive to my help. Problem solved.

Hey, I know taking ownership isn't always easy. Recognising your part in your problems can be uncomfortable and downright confronting at times. However, once you start exercising that muscle, I assure you it does get easier. There's no better time to start than now.

Undesirable Situation	My Part (Action or Behaviour)

Once you know the behaviours and actions, or even inactions, that are contributing to your problems, the final step is to change them. The power is in your hands — it always has been — and now's the time to start using it. You've got this.

FILTERING FOR THE RIGHT FIT

If I take on a client who isn't the right fit, that's on me. I can't blame the client if I didn't adequately assess our compatibility before I agreed to work with them. At the bare minimum, clients must share our values of trust, loyalty, respect, and integrity.

I also pay attention to personality types. To put it bluntly, some clients are more trouble than they're worth. Fortunately, I'm really good at reading people. I've always been able to read people's energy, and it's a skill I further honed when I worked in sales after university. When first meeting someone, I get a feel for them; I pay attention to their rhythm and their vibration, and I can sum up their personality right away. My intuition is rarely wrong. It's a kind of soul-sensing that I've acquired. It's much more than understanding body language or even the words they utter; it's deeper than that — a resonance of their being that I can feel and attune myself to.

Sometimes if my senses don't detect anything strong, I always give the client the benefit of the doubt. I might choose to work with someone for a month at a time and reassess the relationship at the end of each month. If, however, someone does turn out to be a good fit, we can then switch to a more long-term arrangement. If they're unreasonably demanding or derailing the process, I cut them loose, as my time is better spent helping those who actually want what I have to offer, not what they think I should be offering. Of course, I set expectations clearly at the start so there's no excuse for causing trouble when I'm simply following the process we agreed upon.

Ultimately, I want to enjoy who I work with, but I also want my team to enjoy who they work with. When working for other agencies, I was forced to deal with some nightmare clients. Some of them were completely insane. Clearly, there was no filter in place, and the agency was just taking on anyone who walked through the door and could pay the fees. The worst clients were beyond help but if I wanted to keep my job, I had to try to help them anyway, which was a massive waste of time and an unnecessary source of stress. I never want to put anyone else in that position, which is why I'm so selective about who we work with.

Difficult personalities aren't the only things I need to filter out when it comes to potential clients. I also need to ensure a client's business is ready to take full advantage of my services. Sometimes a business owner will come to me all excited about how they want to do SEO and Google Ads, but they're not ready for any of that. They haven't identified the problem they solve or who they solve it for. Essentially, they don't have a clear idea of what they offer, which makes creating a successful SEO or Google Ads campaign near-impossible.

Just because someone isn't ready for my main services, it doesn't mean I can't help them get there. The more clients I turned away because they weren't ready, the more I realised I needed to offer something for smaller businesses, so I created The Growth Movement. Through my online marketing membership, which focuses on business growth through the omnichannel approach, I allow business owners to tap into my knowledge for a fraction of the cost of working with me directly. I see so many business owners who began with a vision to create financial freedom so they could spend more time with their loved ones and doing what they love, only to end up spending much more time in their businesses than they anticipated. Been there, done that. They know they need to grow, but they haven't found the right strategy, and they're not ready to outsource to an agency. Essentially, The Growth Movement is a stepping stone to help business owners get to a point where they're ready to take advantage of our main services. As far as I'm concerned, there's no point taking someone's money for an SEO or Google Ads campaign that won't get great results. I'm all about putting the client first. If I can help them grow their business to a point where they're ready to work with me directly, it's a win for everyone. That doesn't mean they *must* work with me directly once they reach a certain level. Many will simply achieve the growth they want using the strategies in my program.

Either way, before you can build something amazing, you must lay the groundwork. You must approach business growth with a sound strategy. Otherwise you're just setting yourself up to fail.

Stop Pointing Fingers and Take Ownership

1. You have the power. No matter how stuck or powerless you might feel, you have the power to change your situation. In fact, you're the only one who truly does. Once you understand this, there are no limits to what you can achieve.

2. Don't be afraid to fire a client (or end a difficult relationship). As a business owner, you might think you need to serve everyone. You might believe that BS line about the customer always being right when the customer is, in fact, often wrong. I know that firing a client is easier said than done, especially for newer business owners, but your own sanity should always come first. If a relationship is never going to work, you might as well end it now so you can both move on with your lives.

3. Always ensure the right fit. The best way to avoid taking on a, let's say, incompatible client is to filter them out from the start. Set expectations clearly from the outset. Pay attention to red flags. Don't proceed with a relationship that seems like it will be more trouble than it's worth.

The unknown
can lead to new
possibilities,
ideas, and
connections.

AWAKENING THE WARRIOR

3

GET COMFORTABLE WITH UNCERTAINTY

THE REAL JOURNEY BEGINS

In 2018, Kevin and I got married, spending the final part of our honeymoon in Rome. There, we met an American couple who were travelling around Europe with their kid, who was still a baby. I was infatuated with her. She was so beautiful. Kevin and I were making funny faces at each other, trying to get the baby to smile. We were smitten.

On our final night in Rome, we went to a bar called Ted's for cocktails, and I suggested that we start trying for a baby right away. I'd always wanted to be a mum. It was one of my big life goals. At the time, Kevin's dad was quite sick, and having a baby would come with the added bonus of giving him something to fight for.

We started trying in September of 2018. With any luck, by December, I'd soon have a present in my tummy for Christmas. But it seemed that the universe had other plans for us.

I spent the rest of the year setting up my business. Fortunately, once some of my former clients from other agencies caught wind that I was going out on my own, they jumped ship to join me, so I hit the ground running and didn't slow down.

Right before Christmas, my time of the month came, and, much to my disappointment – or really devastation – I realised we weren't getting the present we had hoped for. On Christmas eve, I saw baby announcement after baby announcement appear on social media. While I felt happy for all the soon-to-be parents, each announcement was like a punch in the guts. I decided to take a break from social media and some social events, as all the baby announcements were triggering me. More than anything in life, I wanted to be a mum, and we couldn't seem to make it happen, no matter how hard we tried. My gut told me I had a serious battle ahead of me – and unfortunately it was right.

In February of 2019, I felt the most intense pain in my uterus. I was 2 days late, and I thought I was having a miscarriage. I vomited from the pain, and Kevin suggested calling an ambulance, as I was shaking like a leaf and running a high fever. I ended up getting into a hot bath and breathing through the pain. Eventually, it subsided. *What the hell just happened?* It turned out to be just an extremely bad period.

Two days later, I called my gynaecologist, who suggested we get fertility tested, which we agreed to. On 16 March 2019, we got the results. "I'm sorry," the doctor said, "but the road to having a baby is going to be very complicated." The blood drained from my face, and I felt nauseous as my whole world crumbled. The news hit me like a bus. I hadn't navigated this terrain before, and I wasn't sure what to do, say, or even think.

As I left the doctor's office, I was battling denial and disbelief. *What now?* Although Kevin and I reassured each other that we'd get through it, I fell into a deep depression. For days, I felt extreme pain in my chest, as if my heart were breaking into a million pieces, like fragile shells underfoot on the beach. I cried uncontrollably and kept asking myself, *Why? Why us? Why can't falling pregnant be easy for us like it is for so many others?* At that point, I wasn't ready to accept any responsibility for our situation. I wasn't ready to do the all-important inner work. I simply wanted to know why the universe had chosen to punish us.

SELF-DEVELOPMENT JOURNEY AND AN UNEXPECTED TRIP

At a certain point on our fertility journey, I realised I had a lot of work to do on myself. I couldn't just sit back and expect everything to work out. I still had many inner demons to conquer, as did Kevin.

In the search for answers, I went down the path of self-development: holistic modalities, seminars and workshops, kinesiology, healing groups, somatic therapies, craniosacral therapy, neurofeedback sessions, and reading book after book. I did Tony Robbins seminars, and worked with leading-edge coaches.

I started to face the darkest shadows of my soul. I had nothing to lose and everything to gain in becoming a mum.

Over time, I began to understand that there's a positive and negative side to every situation. Where there's dark, there's also light; you just have to look for it. If we go through life always chasing the positive, we create more negative. The key is to see the beauty in the dark times and the darkness in the beauty, always maintaining balance. We live in a society where we believe that instant gratification is the way to quell our thirst, but it's only a temporary fix. Instead, just as with SEO, in life we must play the long game. We must take the negatives with the positives. They're an unavoidable fact of life.

While all the self-development and inner work was great, I didn't feel like I was quite where I needed to be. I was reading a lot, learning a lot, and doing a lot, but deep down I wasn't totally convinced. I didn't feel like I'd had the big breakthrough I needed. I was putting in the work, and I was close, but I wasn't quite there. Then I discovered psychedelics.

Some of the world's most successful people talk openly about their positive experiences with psychedelics. To quote Steve Jobs, "Taking LSD was a profound experience, one of the most important things in my life. LSD shows you that there's another side to the coin, and you can't remember it when it wears off, but you know it."

Elon Musk and Joe Rogan also claim life-altering experiences. Prince Harry attributes it to helping him deal with his trauma and loss, and famed trauma therapist and psychologist Gabor Maté says psychedelics can alter neural pathways and help people 'reset' their fight-or-flight response and also increase their capacity to regulate emotions. There's still a lot more research to be done in the field of psychedelics and health, but it seems to be increasing in popularity due to its transformative experiences.

As it turned out, my introduction to psychedelics came just at the right time.

Kevin and I had just gone through three failed IUI (intrauterine insemination) cycles, which is the step before trying IVF (in-vitro fertilisation). It felt like the setbacks would never end.

One day, I was at a friend's place, and one of her friends started talking about the positive energy and sense of peace that had come over him.

"What are you talking about?" I asked.

"I had an incredible experience doing magic mushrooms with a shaman."

My intuition nudged me to say, *This is the next step.* My gut was so strong on this. I didn't fully understand what he was talking about or what he had experienced, but at that point I was willing to give anything a go. With the setbacks piling up, I was beginning to think we'd never have kids, and I was trying to find a way to accept that fact. Were psychedelics the answer? I didn't know, but I got the shaman's number and booked a session anyway. What did I have to lose?

I was reassured to know that using psychedelics in therapeutic settings has been shown to help some people process and heal from trauma, and induce spiritual awakenings, and release emotional blocks from the body, particularly when used under the guidance of a trained shaman or medical professional.

In October of 2020, I had my first psychedelic experience with a substance called 'kambo' or 'frog'. It's a poison extracted from a frog that lives deep in the Amazon. In Peru, the substance is used in a healing ritual.

The practitioner administered the kambo to my skin on my meridian lines. Within 20 minutes, my heart was racing, and I was sweating profusely. The medicine was supposed to draw out all my anger, bitterness, and resentment, and I'd purge in one of several ways – either through vomiting, going to the toilet, or sweating it out. For me, it was vomiting. The moment I purged, all the mental chatter stopped. It was surreal.

The goal was to remove as many layers as possible so the mushrooms could do their work. The less there was to peel back, the better. When I finally did the mushrooms, the first thing that came up was shame around my sexuality and femininity. Growing up, I got bullied a lot, and it was something I hadn't quite dealt with, but the mushrooms forced me to confront and overcome it.

Many painful memories surfaced and revealed some deeply embedded trauma. My teenage years were filled with vicious taunts and bullying by other girls. One particular incident scarred me. I was in a beauty pageant, and some girls made up rumours that I was caught in a sexual act with a married man. Although it wasn't true, I was afraid of what others would think. Coming from a broken home, I knew the pain of a family splitting up, so I would have never been with a married man. The rumours cut deep and made me feel cheap. They eroded my self-esteem and damaged my reputation.

When I took mushrooms, I clearly saw the old patterns of low self-worth and the root causes that grew them. It became obvious that my trauma was holding me back and I needed to confront it with self-love and reclaim my femininity and sexual power.

What a liberating experience! Without this awareness, I may never have risen in my full feminine strength and truly owned the beauty of my sexual expression.

A few months later, I did mushrooms a second time, and the trip gave me one of the most profound lessons of my life. I was confronted with the questions of whether Kevin and I were compatible. I saw all the areas where I was already embodying the archetype of a mother. I was a mother to my two dogs, Coco and Milo. I was a mother in my business. I was a loving wife. I realised it didn't matter if Kevin and I couldn't have kids because I was already a mother in so many ways. I allowed myself to feel the love I had for my husband, despite our challenges. I realised that, in frustration, I had been pointing fingers, looking for someone or something to blame. *What's my part in this?* I still hadn't conquered the worst of my inner demons. How could I give everything to a child when I was still fighting so many battles within myself? I couldn't. Finally, everything had been brought to the surface, and the real healing began.

A GLIMMER OF HOPE

While business was booming, things still weren't great on the fertility front. We tried to continue with normal life, but the frequent baby announcements on social media and questions at social gatherings – "So, when are you having kids?" – were a constant reminder of the tough road ahead. Those questions were like daggers, cutting deep to my heart. I'd swallow the lump in my throat and, holding back tears, reply, "We'll wait a while and see what happens." During this time, running my business was a welcomed distraction from what was happening in my personal life.

There were times when I thought our marriage wouldn't last. Kevin and I would distance ourselves from each other so much that we weren't always there for one another. We were both lost in our own pain. Although we both struggled with the reality of the situation, we never fully gave up hope. Through IVF, we continued the fight for what we wanted.

Just before Australia Day in January 2021, we started IVF. The first round failed due to under-stimulation despite so many injections. During a scan, the nurses checked how many eggs would be ready for harvesting. I was told there was only one egg ready for harvesting, so the egg collection was cancelled. Kevin and I got into a huge argument (keep in mind that I was juiced up on raging hormones at this point). Nothing seemed to be going our way.

It turned out the clinic never gave me the right drugs, which resulted in the under-stimulation. It was such a blow – all the injections and psyching myself up emotionally and physically for absolutely nothing.

In February 2021, we started the whole IVF process again. This time they changed the drugs and gave me a higher dose. The scan prior to egg collection was a huge success. I had a total of 20 eggs collected, and on this occasion I hyperstimulated (produced too many eggs). They said I needed to give my body 2 months to heal to ensure it was the right environment for an embryo to attach. I woke up in recovery and saw the number 20 on my hand. The days that followed were intense; every day they gave me an update on how the eggs were fertilised. Some of the eggs were immature due to the hyperstimulation; ten eggs fertilised initially with the frozen sperm. Then, in the days that followed, our numbers dropped. We needed to wait 5 days before the clinic would freeze any embryos to ensure high success of a positive pregnancy. The following day we had nine embryos; the day after that we had seven, and on day 5 we only had three successful embryos suitable for freezing. When they told me we had three embryos, I was shattered. It seemed like a huge number of eggs and such an epic process... ending up with such a low number upset me. I burst into tears and rang Kevin to tell him the news. From then on, I was in limbo waiting for my body to heal before we could do another embryo transfer. The waiting period was excruciating.

Then, after endless waiting periods, multiple failed IUIs, a series of IVF cycles, injecting myself with endless hormones, and an embryo transfer scheduled on 25 April 2021 (ANZAC Day), in May 2021 we found out we were pregnant and finally expecting our baby on 13 January 2022. *Woo hoo!* It had been a long, gruelling journey from first trying for a baby back in 2018 to falling pregnant, but our persistence had paid off. We were absolutely over the moon.

I was so sick with nerves that I didn't feel pregnant... but I was! I went into self-presevation mode and tried to keep a lid on my excitement because we still had a long way to go. I kept having dreams about the baby. In the dream, I couldn't see the baby's face and kept dreaming of dropping the baby on its head.

This frightened me, but I was full of nerves and desperate to be a mum.

At 8 weeks, we had our first scan and learnt that we had lost our little miracle to a silent miscarriage called blighted ovum – a condition where the embryo stops developing. Reluctantly, I proceeded with D and C (dilation and curettage) surgery to remove the remains of our baby. We really thought this was our time, and we never thought miscarriage would also be a part of our journey. We later learnt through extensive testing we had been expecting a baby boy.

Once again, I threw myself into my business, which helped me cope with the pain in my personal life. On the outside, everything looked fine. No one had a clue that, on the inside, I was battling pain and trauma. Honestly, my business was one of my greatest saviours during this time.

A LITERAL BLOODBATH

On 2 August 2021, I was invited as a guest to speak on an Instagram Live for a series 'How to Socialise Online'. That morning, I had a follow-up scan after the D and C to ensure everything was okay. During the scan, they found clots all over my uterus, like a colony of mushrooms growing in a field, along with the remains of the miscarriage.

When I arrived at the office that day, I sat at my desk to clear my inbox. Suddenly, I felt something warm gush down my legs. I looked down and saw a massacre. There was blood everywhere, and to make matters worse, I was wearing light-coloured jeans. During the morning's examination, the clots in my uterus had become dislodged. I thought that by having a silent miscarriage 2 months prior, I had avoided the horrifying experience many women go through, at least physically. Apparently not.

My heart sank. *Oh my god.* Embarrassment coursed through me. *I have an Instagram Live in two hours. What am I going to do?* I wrapped a cardigan around my waist and attempted to flee the office. One of my team tried to ask me something as I rushed out the door, but I was too flustered to respond properly. *Gotta go,* I blurted out. *Be back soon.* Then I was gone.

I literally ran to my car. Careening through the streets, I must have looked like a mad woman behind the wheel. But I had a mission. I didn't have time to think about what had happened. I had an Instagram Live to do, and I had to show up for my business that day. Everything else could wait. After everything that had happened, it was reassuring to see that the warrior within was alive and well.

When I got home, I had a shower, put on some fresh clothes, and drove back to the office. I was able to compartmentalise, put on my brave face and my big-girl pants, and do the Live with the host. I locked the whole bloody experience in a box to deal with later. During the Live, I was hoping and praying I wouldn't have another massacre. *Sonja, please don't bleed again. Please don't bleed again. Please don't bleed again.* Fortunately, I survived the Instagram Live – it actually went great. Who would've thought?

I knew our fertility journey would be challenging, but I couldn't have known just how trying it would be. Relentless uncertainty, chronic stress, and living in hope certainly take their toll on a person and relationship.

INNER WARFARE: AN ACTIVITY TO AWAKEN YOUR WARRIOR

Get Comfortable with Uncertainty

To get comfortable with uncertainty, think about what you can control in life and what you can't control in life. Be honest. **Write them down.**

For example, I can't control what happened in the past, but I can control if I let it still control me. I can't control someone's opinion, but I can control how I respond to them.

What I Can Control	What I Can't Control

What I Can Control	What I Can't Control
....	....
....	....
....	....
....	....
....	....

Now, with the controllables, identify the actions you'll take to ensure you remain in control of them. **Write them down.**

For example, *I can't control what happened in the past, but I can control if I let it still control me* may mean that, instead of ruminating about the past, you'll go to the gym or work on your business instead of wasting time in cyclic thinking patterns that can't actually change anything.

THE UNCERTAINTY OF THE FERTILITY CURSE

Through accepting the lessons of the past, embracing the uncertainty and doing the inner work (with some psychedelic assistance), and healing myself, I was able to put myself in a better mental state for becoming a mum. Each new weapon I added to my arsenal, each challenging dance step I learnt better equipped me for what lay ahead. We were preparing to continue our fertility fight, which meant accepting what I could control and what I couldn't.

The thing is, there's no point wishing for peace on Earth if we're not willing to do the inner work and heal ourselves. It all starts with us. Look at what's going on in the world – it's filled with uncertainty, and many people remain unwilling to look inward. They're afraid of what they might find. However, a warrior knows she must first conquer her inner demons before she can make her mark on the external world. The more we look inward, lean into discomfort, and accept what we can't control, the sooner we'll find inner peace and build the external lives we desire.

I believe that every soul's journey when they come to Earth is about discovering who they really are, and the greatest gift you can give to the universe is to show gratitude and have a healthy relationship with yourself over prioritising your external environment. Through psychedelics, I was able to fall in love with who I really am. Once I felt more at peace internally, things really started to go my way.

On 23 October 2021, we had our second embryo transfer. It was exactly 6 months to the day since the first transfer. This time felt different. Instantly, I knew I was pregnant. Of course, at this point, there was no way to know for sure, but deep down I knew that now was our time.

On the 5 November 2021, we learnt that we were expecting our baby. We knew not to celebrate too early, but I had a good feeling about this one. Like I said, I knew that our time had finally arrived.

Get Comfortable with Uncertainty

1. View uncertainty as a normal part of life. Accept that uncertainty is an inevitable part of the human experience. Remember, it's natural to seek certainty, but it's important to acknowledge that some level of uncertainty will always exist.

2. Control the controllables. There will always be things outside your control. Learn to let go of what you have no control over and focus on what you can control.

3. Reframe uncertainty as opportunity. Instead of seeing uncertainty as a source of concern, view it as a space for growth, creativity, and exploration. The unknown can lead to new possibilities, ideas, and connections.

4. Take small, manageable actions. If you feel overwhelmed by uncertainty, break things down into smaller, actionable steps. Focusing on what you can control, even in small ways, can give you a sense of agency.

5. Stop blaming external forces and face your inner demons. Through psychedelics, I realised my biggest problems weren't coming from external forces. They were the result of inner demons I had yet to conquer. Don't let yours rule your life.

6. Be prepared to show strength when times get tough (more on that later). When I experienced my miscarriage and the resulting office massacre, I could have curled up into a ball, cried, and neglected all my responsibilities. If I did, I'm sure people would have understood. But strength isn't something you should only exercise when it suits you. Real strength is born when we feel most vulnerable.

One of the biggest reasons a harmful pattern continues is because you failed to learn the lesson.

AWAKENING THE WARRIOR

4

IDENTIFY THE LESSONS IN PAST STRUGGLES – THERE'S A POSITIVE IN EVERYTHING

THE EASY LESSON, OR THE HARD LESSON? YOUR CHOICE

Over the years, I've learnt a valuable lesson that I'm now going to pass on to you: if you ignore the lessons life presents you, you're going to get hit with an even bigger lesson later. Didn't learn it the first time, or even the second, third, or fourth? Well, the next time, it's going to hit you even harder, which is why it's so important to pay attention to all the lessons life offers.

It's like the universe whispers to you at first, but if you don't listen, the next time it becomes a little tap or a shove; then if you don't pay attention, that shove becomes a slap in the face. Don't wait for the sledgehammer!

> Your greatest insights will come from your most challenging moments. If you don't learn from them, you've wasted something valuable, and you're destined to repeat the mistakes of the past.

We already know the downsides of repeating harmful patterns, don't we? Part of breaking those patterns is learning the lessons they teach.

For instance, during my pregnancy with our second daughter (more on Willow later), I felt called to take a week off work to recharge, as I was struggling with energy and was surviving on very little sleep due to pregnancy insomnia in the middle of a busy period. I had two massive speaking events scheduled where people were paying me a lot of money to speak, but I trusted my body, took the week off, and postponed the speaking events. On the surface, cancelling those engagements seemed utterly insane. Why would I give up such amazing opportunities? But I knew myself, and I knew my body. I was redlining, overworking myself, pushing towards burnout, and past experiences, past lessons taught me to slow down when the warning light comes on.

As business owners, we're pretty much go, go, go all the time. If you're feeling overworked and overwhelmed, stop what you're doing and take a breath. The daily grind has been glorified so much that we constantly push ourselves to our limits. It's the proven path to success, right? In the short term, maybe. But what about the long term? I learnt the hard way that if you don't slow things down of your own volition, life finds a way to do it for you. Taking time to recharge and reflect isn't just an essential part of self-care. In my experience, it also leads to greater creativity, better problem-solving skills, and increased productivity over time. By pushing yourself to perform, you might be actually hurting your performance.

As Isaac Newton so wisely said, "What goes up must come down." If you're not careful with your time and energy, life will smack you on the head. When doing the dance of life, you can't perform at a high tempo the entire time. It can be a long and gruelling performance, and, to avoid exhaustion, you must alter the intensity when necessary.

Remember – slowing down doesn't mean stopping altogether. The key is to find a healthy balance between working hard enough to achieve your goals while also looking after yourself. I know it's not easy. However, I guarantee that if I ignored previous lessons about overwork, I would've driven myself to burnout, creating an even bigger problem with a harsher lesson attached.

Ultimately, my baby, my health, both physical and mental, were more important than money or a great speaking opportunity. *If I miss out, so what?* Don't let the universe push you around. Do only what's best for you. It's your life, and you have the power.

Fortunately, I was able to reschedule the events rather than having to cancel completely, so it worked out perfectly in the end. If you listen to your intuition, you'll usually know the answer to most questions. *Should I do this? Should I do that?* Your gut, informed by past lessons and outcomes, always knows the answer. But you must be willing to listen.

THE BIRTH OF THE SEARCH QUEEN

Have you ever had a situation go sideways and thought to yourself, *I've been here before?* I have. Plenty of times. When this happens, the questions you need to ask yourself are:

What's the lesson I need to learn?
What could I have done differently?
How will I stop this pattern from repeating?

Growing up, I put a lot of people on pedestals. I looked up to so many people, and it never ended well. **When you put people on pedestals, it's easy to put yourself in a pit.** I kept ending up in the wrong crowd, frequently got stabbed in the back, and struggled to find real friends. For me, the problem stemmed from insecurity and abandonment issues. Because I wanted to be liked, accepted, and to fit in, I didn't feel like I could be myself, which led to more insecurity and me constantly falling on my face. Outwardly, I was doing the dance I thought people wanted to see, regardless of what I felt on the inside, which must have appeared totally unnatural. It certainly felt that way. It wasn't until I really reflected and identified the lesson in past failures that I was able to break the pattern, learning to accept myself wholly. The conditioning we receive at school trains us to blend in with the crowd and not rock the boat. For years, I tried it, and it didn't get me anywhere. When I finally accepted my authentic self and put myself out there, life got a whole lot better.

When I first started my business, I didn't put myself out there at all. I struggled to show the courage of a true warrior, hiding behind my business to avoid facing the fire. However, when I reflected on the past and realised that suppressing my authentic self had never done me any favours – in fact, it had only caused problems – I knew what I had to do. It was time to finally put myself out there by launching my own personal brand to complement my business.

When I first set up my business, it was called 'The Marketing Republiq'. I liked that the word 'republic' centred on doing the right thing. However, 'The Marketing Republic' name wasn't available, so I switched out the C for a Q and went with that. In the early days, the business offered a vast range of marketing services;

however, my passion was always with Google, so I rebranded to The Search Republic in 2022, as it felt more aligned with Google and the results we were getting for our clients, and my personal brand.

We decided to offer only Google services rather than all marketing services. As the saying goes, when you're a jack-of-all-trades, you're a master of none. The power is in the niche.

Before the rebrand, you could be forgiven for confusing The Marketing Republiq with any other typical marketing agency. Once again, I was trying to blend in with the crowd. I truly believe my purpose in business is to help other businesses grow on Google. So many business owners find SEO and Google Ads overwhelming, which can turn them off even trying to make it work. Often, they've been burnt in the past, blaming Google for poor results or saying it isn't worth it. Of course, I knew differently, and, in order to help others understand the often-untapped potential of Google, I had to put myself out there, start to build trust, and educate my audience around the smoke and mirrors that surround Google for businesses, focusing on debunking the myths and false promises. In the industry, trust was the missing link. To cut through the noise, I had to develop my personal brand and injcct that human element into what I do. Essentially, I was humanising the process, explaining all the technical jargon in a language people could understand.

When the COVID pandemic hit, the warrior within was growing restless, and I knew it was time to pivot to a personal brand. No more hiding behind a business name. So in 2020, I launched my personal brand, Sonja The Search Queen. Times were uncertain, and competition in the industry was fierce. If I didn't do something to stand out in the crowd, I risked looking like every other agency and getting lost in the noise. I couldn't waste too much time and money promoting The Marketing Republiq (now The Search Republic) in such a saturated market. Funnily enough, I've since noticed competitors producing content similar to mine. Do I care? Honestly, no. I get it – it works. I'm all for businesses adding value for their clients. As Oscar Wilde said, "Imitation is the sincerest form of flattery," and I'm sincerely flattered that my competitors have seen fit to imitate me.

To market myself and my services, I chose to take a more human approach, letting people get to know, like, and trust me. Marketers sometimes get a bad rap, and I wanted to show that I was pushing for positive change in the industry. One of my goals is to regulate the industry so we can start rebuilding that all-important trust across the board. I know it will piss off some people (that is, shady marketers), but marketing shouldn't be a shady business.

So, how exactly did I earn the 'Search Queen' label? At one agency, I was managing over 150 clients on my own, with very little support. "Oh, Sonja's the Search Queen," people would say. The label stuck and when the time came to launch my personal brand, I knew exactly what it would be. In 2020, my personal 'Sonja The Search Queen' brand was officially born.

As you might have guessed, listening to my intuition, acting on the lessons of the past, and putting myself out there authentically had a massively positive outcome. I was able to build a stronger connection with my audience, better educate more people and solve their problems, and eventually share our fertility journey, letting others experiencing the same challenges know they're not alone. I think it's important to show both sides of life, as it's not all plus plus. It's the balance of both positive and negative. Surprise surprise, the majority of my clients are women, which I feel is due to my fertility advocacy being a part of my personal brand.

HOT TIPS FOR DEVELOPING YOUR PERSONAL BRAND

When I was developing Sonja The Search Queen, I learnt many lessons along the way. I did some things right, but I also did some things wrong. In the beginning, fear, anxiety, self-doubt, and impostor syndrome ruled my thoughts, which I'll talk more about later. Right now, I'm going to give you my best tips for developing your own personal brand based on the lessons I've learnt.

If you don't think you have a personal brand, I'm sorry, but you're wrong. Essentially, your personal brand is what people say about you when you're not in the room. It's how you present to, and are perceived by, the outside world.

It's time to take your personal brand to the next level. Ready for it? Let's go. Here are my hottest tips for developing your own personal brand:

- **Focus on the vision, NOT the money.** When you make

your brand about the money, you limit your vision, and people feel it. But when you focus on what you're here to do and what you can contribute to the world, the money comes automatically as a reflection of the lives you've touched.

- **Do the inner work.** You can't have a successful personal brand if you're not willing to do the work within yourself. When you're not being genuine, people feel it. People's BS detectors are so sensitive online. They're used to being manipulated. Anyone who follows me knows I've done a serious amount of personal development work, but I'm still a work in progress. We all are. If we're not growing, we're dying. The better you know who you really are on the inside, the more people you attract on the outside. It's that simple.

- **Video yourself and practise.** When you put yourself out there, you have to be comfortable watching and listening to yourself. For some of us, it doesn't come easily. When I first started hearing myself back, I would cringe at the sound of my own voice. But the more I did it, the more I overcame it, and the more I actually liked what I was hearing. We're conditioned to cringe when we hear our own voices played back to us, but, with a little persistence, we can break that conditioning.

- **Get over yourself.** Newsflash – it's not about you. It's about who you can serve. Stop making it about you and your issues, and focus on how you can help.

- **Challenge yourself.** To grow as a person and a brand, you need to put yourself in situations that make you uncomfortable. With every new step you take, you'll likely have some doubt and even fear. It's normal. The key is to get comfortable with the uncomfortable. For example, I now reframe my fear as excitement.
- **Be consistent.** Show up for your audience even on the tough days and especially when you don't want to. We all have our daily struggles, and your audience is made up of regular people just like you. When you show that you're just like them – because you are – it makes you more relatable. You don't need to project the perfect social media persona. In fact, it can do more harm than good. Authenticity is a much more effective and honest approach. But the biggest piece of advice I'd like to give here is share your learnings when you overcome a challenge to avoid 'trauma dumping' on your audience.
- **Hire a coach.** Don't take advice from anyone unqualified to give it. Instead, find someone who has been there, done that, and can guide you on your own journey. But you must be prepared to do the work. A coach can't do it for you. If you don't do the work or follow your coach's advice, the lessons will catch up with you eventually. It's best to learn them the easy way.
- **Add value.** Use your personal brand to help connect others. If people within your circle will benefit from an introduction, then make the invitation and connect people.

Focus on strengthening the relationships within your business circle, add value, more value, and even more. Always go that extra mile.
- 🔥 **Be humble in the pursuit of success.** In order to remain relatable and likeable, while keeping your feet on the ground and staying focused on your goals, don't fall into the trap of thinking you're better than anyone (especially as you start to become successful). It can hurt your success.

There you have it – all the lessons I had to learn the less-than-easy way. I'm giving them to you now so you can skip the hard part and dive right into building your personal brand. Think of it as taking a brand-building shortcut. Now that you have the knowledge, it's time to do the work.

LET'S TALK ABOUT THE C WORD

When building your personal brand or business, you need to be online. With very few exceptions, there's no way around it. If you're not online, you don't exist to the average consumer, and that will only become truer as time goes on. Nowadays, it's no longer enough to have a slick website, although it is encouraged. You must also have a strong social media presence if you want your brand and business to reach its full potential and a wide audience. Of course, social media is just one of the 15 channels you'll need to focus on to grow your business. I cover each one in depth in The Growth Movement. Let me be clear – social media shouldn't be your entire marketing strategy. For maximum growth, other channels need attention too. Social media is simply one part of a larger strategy.

To be effective on socials, you need something very specific. What is it? I'm talking about the C word. Charm? Class? Charisma? While these things will help, none of them are the C word we're looking for. I'm talking about CONTENT.

Content is the mac and cheese of the internet. Hear me out. It's delicious; we can't get enough of it and if we consume too much, we'll probably get sick (but we'll always come back for more). That's my analogy, and I'm sticking with it.

When whipping up your content marketing feast (your digital mac and cheese), you must use the right ingredients. But how do you know which ingredients are correct? While everyone seems to have their own recipe, few are willing to share it. But don't stress – I'm going to share my not-so-secret recipe right now.

Firstly, we need to understand that not all content – not every ingredient – serves the same purpose. While it may all look the same on the box, results will vary, from driving traffic to collecting data. Therefore, it's crucial to have a content marketing recipe that maximises the effectiveness of each ingredient for the purpose it serves.

So, what are the essential ingredients for a good bowl of content, and what purpose do they serve? Let's find out.

1. **SEO-friendly web copy.** Includes on-page SEO (everything on a website, including blogs), off-page SEO (off-site content and links that drive traffic to a website), and technical SEO (web coding). Each category comes with an extensive list of deliverables you must meet for the best results.
2. **Lead magnets.** Some examples include free checklists, training, and ebooks, which provide an opportunity to offer value to your audience and generate leads now and into the future. While they take more time and effort to produce than many other content forms, once they're completed, you'll reap the benefits for years to come.
3. **Case studies.** The proof is in the pudding (or in this case, the pasta). There's nothing as valuable to potential clients as showing how you solved a problem for a current client. Ideally, they'll see themselves in others you've helped and realise you can help them too.
4. **Videos.** Our brains are ravenous for moving images and, at the same time, have increasingly short attention spans, so creating short-form content from longer video pieces is a great way to draw people in.

SEO-friendly web copy, lead magnets, case studies, videos – here we have the four essential ingredients for our content feast. That doesn't mean you can't season the dish with other ingredients. However, if you're looking for a simple way to get started, this four-ingredient recipe will do the trick.

INNER WARFARE: AN ACTIVITY TO AWAKEN THE WARRIOR

Identifying the Lessons in Past Struggles

I truly believe there's a positive, a lesson, a nugget of wisdom in every difficult situation. Whenever something seemingly bad happens, ask yourself, *What's the lesson here? Where's the magic? How's this trying to bring me back into balance?* Although it can be difficult to see at times, even our most traumatic moments can gift us powerful lessons.

As JR Rim said, **"Sunflowers end up facing the sun, but they go through a lot of dirt to find their way there."**

All right, this next part isn't going to be easy. It's time to harness that warrior spirit and think back to the most difficult moments in your life, which will likely also be the most traumatic. Have you identified some? **Write them down.** Now I want you to turn inward, and don't fear what you might find. We're searching for lessons here, not aiming to relive past trauma. What are the positives, the lessons attached to each difficult experience? **Write them down.** Easy to say, I know, but not always easy to do. Remember, every experience has a plus and a minus. Too often, we only focus on the negative, letting the experience hold us back. Instead, we can identify the positive and use it to move us forward. The positives *are* in there. They're in everything. It's the law of the universe.

For example, when my dad left when I was 7 years old, I was hurt, confused, angry. I didn't understand how he could leave his family behind. Him leaving was a traumatic event from my past, which I'll discuss more in depth later, and it was a tough one to confront and analyse. But in order to grow stronger, wiser, and move forward in life, a warrior must be willing to shine a light on the most challenging aspects of her past. While we can't change the past, we can certainly learn from it. So, for **event, situation, or experience**, I'd write: *Dad leaving.*

Now, it took me a while to learn the lesson concealed in this experience. I had to not only learn a lot about myself and my dad but also our family history. I learnt about intergenerational trauma and how it can carry through the generations until someone steps up, takes ownership, and chooses to break the cycle. So, the **lesson learnt**, which admittedly took a while to learn and understand, was: *Intergenerational trauma is persistent and destructive, and if I don't break the cycle, it will continue.*

As a soon-to-be mother, this was a powerful and confronting lesson to learn. If I couldn't reconcile with my hurt inner child (more on that later), I risked passing on the trauma to my own kids in some form or another. I had learnt the lesson so my children wouldn't have to.

Event, Situation, or Experience	Lesson Learnt

Looking inward, examining past adversities, and identifying the golden nuggets (the lessons) they provide is the first part of the process. The next part is to identify and *remember* those lessons and then live them every day.

Personally, journalling helps me remember past lessons and identify new ones. Using pen and paper to put your thoughts into physical words allows you to examine them without feeling attached to them. Basically, it gives you an objective perspective. It can be very insightful and therapeutic. If you're not already journalling, I say give it a go. You might be (pleasantly) surprised at the results.

×✦××✦××✦×

DIGGING TO MY ROOTS

In order to fully appreciate where we are in life, we must acknowledge where we've come from, both in our own lives and ancestrally. A warrior seeks to understand her history, as it paves the path to the present and beyond. The past is full of powerful lessons that we would be much better to acknowledge than to repeat. For better or worse, we're the sum of everything that came before us.

To better understand myself, my personality, and where I've come from, I plan to visit Germany once this book launches. I've already spent some time in Munich, but I want to do a deeper dive into the culture. Even though it's not necessarily my culture, it's still a part of me. I'm so German it's not even funny, and I don't want to deny that part of myself. Instead, I want to own it, just like everything else. But I didn't always feel this way.

When I was younger, I rebelled against my German identity. In school, I dropped German as a subject to focus on French, and I changed the spelling of my name from Sonja with a J to Sonia with an I. I didn't want to be associated with Germany in any way. I wanted to fit in.

It may or may not surprise you to learn that I was a troublesome teenager. I'm sure Mum would agree. At 16 years old, I'd frequently climb out my bedroom window to go to parties and nightclubs when I was meant to be babysitting my younger sister, Linda. I'd turn my phone off when Mum realised I was gone, and she would drive around town looking for me. I really put her through the ringer.

Even after Dad left and I gave her hell, she still managed to handle everything with such grace, keeping all the balls in the air, smashing every life goal she put her mind to, and demonstrating true resilience at every turn. I most certainly get my strength, female empowerment, determination, and resilience from her. She even put me and my sisters into counselling at a young age to ensure we were expressing our emotions in healthy ways. Because of Mum, I know what unconditional love looks like. She showed us what it means to love your children more than anything else in the world. Because of this, I'm able to love at the highest level. Everything she has done for me over the years has made me into the woman I am today. My mum isn't just my best role model; she's also my hero. She has a warrior's heart like no other.

Once I became successful, my dad made the comment, "You must have got your business mind from me."

"Hold on a second," I said. "Don't you take credit for that. I'm where I am today because I watched Mum never give up. I saw what real resilience looks like."

Dad said, "Yeah… you're probably right."

Damn right I'm right.

While Mum was the best role model I could have asked for, she couldn't provide all the answers. Growing up, I had so many questions about my identity, my personality, and where I had come from. When Dad left, finding answers to those questions wasn't easy. As I grew and matured, I realised that if I wanted to understand myself, I needed to have a relationship with my dad. Even though his leaving had hurt me, I needed him in my life in some capacity. I needed him there to help fill the gaps in my understanding of my own identity.

EXPRESSING MY UNTOLD GRATITUDE

For Christmas 2023, I wrote Mum a letter to show my gratitude for everything she has done for me and taught me over the years. Words of affirmation are her 'love language', so she appreciated the letter. I even had my sister frame it so Mum could sit it on her bedside table. I didn't want to leave anything unsaid.

If you're curious to know what I wrote, you're in luck, because I've included the entire letter right here.

> To my fabulous mum,
>
> I wanted to give you some words from my heart about how much you mean to me. I really want and need you to know from the bottom of my heart that I am everything I am because of you. Thank you for everything you have done for me throughout my life. I would not be where I am without you.
>
> I've watched you from a distance my entire life put your kids before yourself. You also taught me to never give up no matter how hard things can be. You rose to the challenge every time to be the best version of yourself.
>
> You taught me what it means to be truly resilient. You were the best role model to me. Your determination and grit are something I possess because of you. You did whatever it took to show I could do anything I put my mind to and I could be anyone I wanted to be.
>
> Thank you for all the sacrifices you made for us to put us through school. Thank you for the wonderful memories from our childhood. I loved our summers in Ballybunion, our Christmases, the picnics on the sitting room floor watching Eurovision and Glenroe, the Saturday night pizza after mass, the movie nights where

we rented our videos from Boherbee video shop, and of course our Sundays in Muckross. They stand out as the highlights of my childhood.

The strong independent woman I am is because of you, and I'm eternally grateful for you. I do not see I lacked anything in my life, nor did I want anything growing up. We always had what we needed, and that was more than enough. I am the woman I am today because of everything that you've done. I am a reflection of all your hard work.

Side by side, oceans apart, mother and daughter will always be connected by the heart.

I love you with all my heart, and I always will.

Your loving daughter, Sonja
xxx

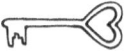

THERE'S ALWAYS A LESSON

By examining the past and identifying the lessons in past struggles, we can avoid repeating the same destructive, clunky, fruitless dance moves that aren't impressing anyone, especially not the warrior within. Have you ever found yourself in an unpleasant situation that seems somehow familiar? *I feel like I've been here before,* you might think. If you really think about it, you might identify a point in your past when you were in the same situation.

The question is, what did you learn from it? If you find yourself repeating the same old pattern, it means you haven't learnt the lesson. Period. I'm fortunate in many ways to have a photographic memory. I can recall exact events, conversations, numbers, dates in vivid detail. When a negative situation arises, I can easily match it to a similar one from my past; then I ask myself, *What's the lesson I failed to learn?*

So, next time you find yourself in an unpleasant situation that seems all too familiar, think back to past events and ask yourself, *What's the lesson I failed to learn?* Because there's always a lesson, and the sooner you learn it, the sooner you can move forward.

> The key is to find a healthy balance between working hard enough to achieve your goals while also looking after yourself.

Identify the Lessons in Past Struggles – There's a Positive in Everything

1. Never push yourself to burnout. Overworking yourself may get short-term results – then again, it may not – but it will also create long-term consequences. It's okay to take a break when necessary. In fact, I encourage it. You'll perform much better if you take a more balanced approach to your work.

2. Listen to your gut. Intuitively, you know all of your past lessons, even if you can't consciously recall them. When in doubt, go with your gut. Most of the time, it will be right, even if you don't know exactly why.

3. Put yourself out there. Don't be afraid to stand out in the crowd. In business, you won't get far if you're simply blending in with everyone else. To stand out, you must stand up, present yourself authentically, and let the world get to know the real you.

4. Look for the lessons in past struggles. We often miss important lessons along the way, but that doesn't mean we can't examine the past and try to identify them now. Better now than never.

5. Harmful pattern repeating? Look for the lesson. One of the biggest reasons a harmful pattern continues is because you failed to learn the lesson. If you keep finding yourself in the same unpleasant situation, ask yourself, *What's the lesson I need to learn?*

We can't appreciate
light without darkness.
Real strength comes
from facing the
darkness head on.

AWAKENING THE WARRIOR

5

MASTER YOUR MENTAL DIALOGUE

TAKE CONTROL OF THE NARRATIVE

Mastering your mental dialogue and taking control of your inner narrative is the journey of becoming your own best friend. It's about examining your thoughts about yourself and asking, *Would I say that to my best friend?* If the answer is no, you then need to figure out why you're treating yourself so harshly. Life will continue to throw down the gauntlet until your last breath. The challenges never stop; they simply change. As you awaken the warrior within, mental dialogue mastery is a must. As Gabrielle Bernstein said, "Each thought you have informs your energy, and your energy manifests into your experiences. Your thoughts and energy create your reality."

How can you effectively face life's battles when you're simultaneously fighting a war inside your head? You can't. It's that simple. Channel that energy elsewhere. Easier said than done, I know.

Even when you know what to look out for, the negative self-talk can still creep in. I often catch myself falling into the mental dialogue trap, treating myself poorly. I might start the day fine, waking up on the right side of the bed, but something during the day might trigger me, sending me into a negative thought spiral. The quicker you catch it and figure out why your mindset has shifted, the quicker you can get back on good terms with yourself.

We often tell ourselves stories, and those stories aren't always true. When you actively watch your thoughts, you notice the story you're telling yourself. Is it true? Are you being a good friend to yourself? Once you identify those renegade thoughts or beliefs, the next step is to take control and start writing a better story for yourself. For some of us, it can be a constant battle.

Years after I thought I had mastered my mental dialogue, I was proven wrong. I was in the process of creating a new program in my business, and I noticed a whole lot of limiting beliefs resurface that I experienced when I first started The Search Republic. I thought I had put them all to rest, but nope. There they were again.

Wow, okay, I thought. *It's time to practise what I preach. This is just my ego trying to protect me. I've been here before. I've overcome this before.* Essentially, it's about being your own therapist and guiding yourself through those limiting beliefs and false narratives.

Most of my negative self-talk stems from the self-esteem issues I developed in childhood. On my mission to fit in, I often found myself in situations where I didn't belong. I'd end up in the company of certain people who would send my thoughts spiralling. It became a repeating pattern. On further examination, I was able to identify what it was about those people that made me think negatively about myself. Next, it was my job to remove those types of people from my life. Eventually, I got the lesson, taking back control of the narrative in the process.

CULTIVATING THE RIGHT MINDSET AROUND FERTILITY

For me, one of the toughest things to do was to master my mental dialogue around my fertility journey. Mastering your mind when anxiety and fear go haywire can be super challenging. When it came to having children, I originally figured that we would try for a few months and boom – I would get pregnant and live happily ever after. Kind of like a feel-good movie or a glossy parenting magazine... you know the type – a beautiful woman easily gets pregnant and spends endless hours rubbing her growing belly and gazing at it in awe.

What I came to realise is the harsh fact – it doesn't happen like that for many people, and I was one of those people. For some of us, the struggle to fall pregnant can be a long and difficult battle.

> **In fact, 1 in 6 couples have trouble getting pregnant.[6]**

Even in the most challenging moments of our fertility journey, my inner knowing told me I was destined to be a mum, but I had to work to control my mental dialogue. I could have easily fallen into the shame trap, but there was nothing to be ashamed about. If I was going to bring this baby into the world, I had to have the right mindset. I had to be real about my situation.

These days, many babies aren't born naturally. It has been that way for a while now. As a woman, it's not uncommon to feel shame around struggling to fall pregnant. We feel like our bodies have failed us. But guess what? That's not always the case. Shocking, I know.

A recent study on infertility and fertility revealed that:

- **In one-third of infertile couples, the problem is with the man.**
- **In one-third of infertile couples, the problem can't be identified or is with both the man and woman.**
- **In one-third of infertile couples, the problem is with the woman.**[7]

Why do I speak so openly about our fertility journey? Because no one else seems to be discussing a very common societal problem. **There's so much stigma around infertility, and ignoring the reality of the situation only feeds that stigma.** It perpetuates the belief that women only create babies naturally, when it just isn't the case anymore. Modern medicine grants the opportunity to have kids to those who, in the past, wouldn't have been able to conceive. It's truly amazing, and infertility and going through IVF isn't something to be ashamed of. It's something to be celebrated. I firmly believe that modern medicine has its place in society. Heck, I wouldn't have my babies if it wasn't for modern medicine, but I don't believe it's the answer to everything.

CONQUERING INNER DEMONS

During our fertility journey, I had to face my inner demons and the shadow parts of my soul. I was forced to dig deep and bring it all into the light where it could be examined. Until that happened, I knew my child wouldn't be ready to come Earthside, because I wasn't ready.

When we had the first embryo transfer, we were so full of doubt and anxiety. We still had demons to conquer. Funnily enough, my biggest battles in life have taken place within. I knew we were destined to be parents, but the timing wasn't right. I firmly believe we lost our baby because we still had a lesson to learn. I know others may not subscribe to this spiritual viewpoint, and that's okay, but for me, this intuitive insight felt right. Our journey was coming together but just not yet.

When we had the second embryo transfer, my inner knowing told me it was going to work – and it was right. The anxiety was gone. The negative self-talk had quieted. Our time had finally come.

Thanks to our fertility journey, I was forced to examine those deep dark parts of myself that were holding me back and forcing me to repeat the same patterns over and over. If it weren't for all that forced self-development, I wouldn't have the business, marriage, friends, confidence, or pride in myself that I have today. If you're struggling with anything in life, don't let it stop you in your tracks. Instead, use it to grow so you can overcome it and move forward.

The warrior views every barrier as an opportunity to hone her strength and resilience.

> To get to the light, you must go through the tunnel of darkness. The warrior isn't afraid of the dark. She knows that if there is darkness, there must also be light. We can't have light without darkness.

We can't *appreciate* light without darkness. Real strength comes from facing the darkness head on, not retreating when times get tough, and always looking for the light.

VANQUISH IMPOSTER SYNDROME FOR GOOD

When I first started my business, I was so full of doubt, and I suffered from imposter syndrome. *What makes you think you can do this? Why would anyone come to you? What if they find out you're not as good as they think you are?* Impostor syndrome makes us doubt our abilities, no matter how qualified or capable we are.

Even though at the time I had a master's degree in marketing, 15 years of experience (now 20 years), and had proven myself in the industry, my mental dialogue wasn't talking me up. It was talking me down, and I was questioning all of my past wins. Some self-doubt is natural — it's how our ego tries to protect us — but giving in to impostor syndrome can prevent us from reaching our goals and achieving our dreams.

To overcome the doubt, I realised I had to challenge my self-belief and limits (the limits my inner detractor was determined to convince me were real). I absolutely love this quote by author Price Pritchett: "If you must doubt something, doubt your limits." You're not the voice in your head, and you don't have to listen to any of that negative self-talk. Choose to doubt your limits, not your capabilities.

When I first started The Search Republic, I didn't even have a website. An SEO and Google Ads expert without a website… yeah, not a good look, but the reality was that I was playing under the radar. Sure, I had a big list of clients from day one, but still the negative self-talk crept in, and I refused to put myself out there. *Who do you think you are? No one's going to listen to you. What makes you think you can run a business?* Part of overcoming the doubt was getting my shit together, building a real business, and shifting my focus to helping my clients, because it's not all about you. It's about the people you want to help.

Let's be real — not everyone will like what you're doing, and some of the criticism will come from external sources. If you aren't ruffling a few feathers along the way, you're likely playing it too safe, and it might be time to step out of your comfort zone. The path of pursuing your biggest dreams can be uncomfortable.

If it wasn't, everyone would be doing it, and so many choose to play it safe. Getting comfortable with being uncomfortable is key to success.

> Always remember that people's
> opinions of you don't pay the bills.

When I launched my personal brand, the self-doubt and impostor syndrome resurfaced. I was putting myself out there, no longer hiding behind a business name and logo. But I had been through this before – I had learnt this part of the dance – and I recognised the pattern. When you feel self-doubt and your mental dialogue is talking you down, take a breath and remember how far you've come. You've earned all of your accomplishments, and you deserve everything you have and more.

Remember, the key is to be your own best friend. As your friend, what would you tell yourself in these situations? When you speak to yourself from a place of love, you'll only ever get the truth, and the truth will propel you forward to the success you deserve.

MONEY – A DIRTY WORD

With success often comes wealth – and I don't mean spiritual wealth. I'm talking money. Cold hard cash. I know that some people view money as a negative, and often destructive, force in the world, and I get it. They see money as the root of all evil. When the cash starts to flow, their mental chatter may try to convince them they should feel guilty for their success, especially if they've come from a disadvantaged background. They may believe that the rich are all selfish and full of themselves, and they don't want to be associated with them. But I'm here to tell you that you don't need to view wealth in a negative light. At a certain point, it starts to provide something very valuable: choice.

Like it or not, we live in a society fuelled by money. It's almost up there with oxygen. Without it, living a healthy and satisfying life is difficult (for most people). I'm not saying money should be your primary focus – it shouldn't. When we do something just for the money, the passion isn't there, and we create inner turmoil. However, if you can generate wealth while doing what you love, you've got nothing to feel guilty about. You can then use that money to create a bigger impact and finance your dream life, whatever that looks like to you.

There was once a time in my life when I tied money to my self-worth. I was earning good money and had erroneously created a mind-pattern around my purchasing power. I was spending mindlessly and weaving my worth into high-end fashion, designer clothes, and nice cars instead of real assets like my intelligence and entrepreneurial skills. Luckily, I noticed this pattern and began the work to untie my sense of self-worth associated with money and spending. I challenged myself to sit in the present moment more and think about the 'energy' of my real worth rather than tying it to how good I looked in my designer threads or what car I drove. I formed new mental patterns about the currency I gave to others in terms of love, support, care, and leadership. I also realised I worked for freedom, not money.

Some will say that wealth and spiritual growth aren't connected, but I disagree. It's not that money can buy spiritual growth – it can't. But the more we evolve spiritually, the more money shows up in our lives. Money simply amplifies more of what you are. The more money you have, the more choice you have. It's a hard fact of modern life. Do you want your life limited by your financial situation? Of course not. To create the life I imagined, I needed to generate a certain amount of wealth. How did I do it? I followed my gut, leant into my passion, and worked hard to build a powerful business and brand. See, it wasn't money I was chasing; it was freedom. Money was simply a tool to get it, a means to an end, and a warrior uses every tool at her disposal.

Wouldn't you prefer to be in control of where you're going in life? Without money, you're sitting on a river in a canoe, letting the current take you wherever it pleases. It may seem okay at first, but you won't ultimately end up where you want to go. However, if you have a paddle (money), you're in control of your journey and can steer your canoe wherever you want it to go. You're making things happen instead of letting them happen to you.

Even if you don't need all that wealth for yourself, you can still use it to create a positive impact for others. Giving is an important part of the human experience. It's one of the reasons why we're here, and few things feel better than giving to and helping another human being. When you have money, you don't have to be selfish or full of yourself like the classic rich stereotype.

Instead, you can use your wealth for the greater good. Is there a cause you're passionate about? For example, one of the biggest goals on my vision board is to work with disadvantaged kids all over the world. So many children grow up without any wealth, without many choices. In extreme cases, bettering their situations without some money behind them is near-impossible, especially those in less-privileged countries than Australia. However, with the right support – financial and educational – disadvantaged kids can pull themselves out of poverty and create the lives they want to live. Success isn't something to be hoarded.

Through the work I'm planning, I can make the world a better place and leave a legacy that long outlasts me. Stopping, looking back, and offering a hand to help others is something we can all do once we achieve our own success. In the grand scheme, the 'fuck you, I got mine' attitude that some well-off people have doesn't make a lot of sense and is in fact more destructive than they realise.

> **We're all connected, and by helping others you're also helping yourself. In the same sense, by hurting others or keeping them down, you're also hurting yourself. It all comes back to us in the end.**

Money can bring out the worst in people, but it also has the potential to bring out the best. It all comes down to choice.

IT ALL STARTS WITH A VISION

I'm a huge advocate for the power of vision boards. It's a big part of my life. I'm a very visual person, so when it comes to setting my goals, nothing imprints into my brain more than an image or detailed visual. Sure, I'll journal and write things down, but it's the visuals that really stick in my mind. According to research, people who use vision boards are twice as confident about achieving their goals than non-users.[8] And 82 percent of small business owners who used a vision board from the start of their journey report that they have accomplished more than half of their goals.[9]

When you visualise your goals, you activate your reticular activating system (RAS), a bundle of nerves responsible for processing sensory stimuli, among other tasks.[10] When you activate your RAS through visualisation or actually seeing your goals on a vision board, you indicate to your brain what it needs to focus on, which prompts your subconscious to find ways to reach those goals and turn your vision into reality.

When I write my vision statement, I always ensure the visuals on my vision board support the words, ensuring my conscious and subconscious minds are on the same page. It's important that the clarity of your vision ties in with the clarity of your vision board.

Being realistic about when you want to achieve your goals is also important. For example, wanting $50 million in your bank account by next year is likely unachievable unless you're already close to that target. Why set yourself up for failure? Sure, you could win the lotto and get the cash that way, but the odds aren't in your favour. **Plenty of people want to win the lottery, but they're not even taking the first and simple step of actually buying a lotto ticket. If you put something on your vision board, you must take the steps to achieve it. Don't expect the universe to hand it to you.**

Your visual goal provides your subconscious mind with a destination, but you'll still need to consciously move towards it. While you should be realistic with your goals, you should also ignore any unfounded limitations you've placed upon yourself or society has placed upon you. They aren't real. When it comes to the vision for your life, you're allowed to dream big. If others have achieved it, you can too. Don't submit to false limitations. Instead, shatter them and prove the doubters (even if one of them happens to be the voice in your head) wrong.

At the very least, a vision board provides clarity on what you want in life, which makes it easier to avoid people and situations that threaten to pull you in the wrong direction. At its best, a vision board is a winning lotto ticket. If you're realistic with your goals and willing to work for them, you'll hit the jackpot every time.

OBLITERATING OBJECTIONS (FROM YOURSELF)

When it comes to chasing goals, unfounded objections from the fearful little voice in your head can threaten to talk you into giving up or not trying at all – but you don't need to listen. Are you actively questioning your proposed limitations (the ones you place on yourself)? Or are you accepting them as fact? Perhaps you're ready to start a business, make a career change, or take your business to the next level, but, instead of cheering you on, that pesky little voice is filling your head with objections.

Are there any limiting beliefs that are holding you back? Are you questioning these beliefs? If not, why not? You know they're not true, right? It's just your ego trying to protect you and keep you small. They're total BS. The sooner you accept it, the sooner you can start moving towards your goals.

The best time to obliterate those objections, those limiting beliefs is *now*. When we hold a set of beliefs for a long time, they tend to form part of the perception we have of ourselves, regardless of how accurate they are. Our personal reality then becomes our personality. Often, we inherit our limiting beliefs from childhood. Because they've been with us for so long, perhaps most of our lives, breaking them requires serious effort and persistence. You're probably not going to break a lifelong belief overnight, although it would be nice. Our limiting beliefs and the objections they produce are BS stories we tell ourselves. The key is to take control and change the narrative. It's your life we're talking about here, and you're the author of your story.

Limiting beliefs come in all shapes, sizes, and flavours. When I was first considering going out on my own, several objections threatened to hold me back:

- I don't have enough time.
- I don't know how to run a business.

- It's not the right time.
- I can't do it alone.
- I'm not good enough.
- I don't deserve success.
- People won't like me.
- I'll look stupid.
- I'll be judged.
- I'll fail.
- I have no business support network.
- There's too much competition.

Do any of those sound familiar? I know I'm not alone in having these thoughts. Can you imagine if I had listened to them? I wouldn't be running a successful business; I wouldn't be The Search Queen, and honestly I probably wouldn't be content with the life I was living.

If I had dealt with these baseless, internal objections sooner, I would have started my business sooner. Instead, I hesitated, ultimately stifling my potential until I felt I was ready.

> **The thing is, you may never feel ready, but that doesn't mean you're not. You just need to take that first scary step and back yourself 100 percent.**

I'll ask again: Are there any limiting beliefs that are holding you back? It's time to identify all the false beliefs and BS objections and remove them from your thought process. You deserve the very best life has to offer. The sooner you accept this, the sooner you'll get it.

False Belief	How Is It Holding You Back?

WHEN YOU'RE STUCK IN A FUNK

Even after doing all the self-development work in the world, you're still going to have bad days. Hey, I'm sure even Gandhi woke up on the wrong side of the bed every now and then. If you find yourself in a funk, failing to do anything about it can cause your thoughts to spiral, and you may end up carrying around that negative mindset for the entire day, or longer.

Personally, when it feels like the world is crumbling around me, I find it harder than ever to get myself out of a funk. On those days, it helps to remind myself that I'm in control of my thoughts, even if it feels like something else is taking over. If you let the negative thoughts win, it's not just your wellbeing that can suffer but your business too.

In 2014, Harvard Business Review interviewed leaders about different states of mind and how each one impacts their performance. It probably won't shock you to learn that 94 percent of respondents said calm, happy, and energised states of mind translated to higher levels of effectiveness and performance.[11] Clearly, mindset matters.

I'm a *huge* advocate of putting yourself first. I know it's not always easy, especially when you have a business, family, and friends to consider. However, if you try to pour from a near-empty cup, everyone goes thirsty. It's up to you to fill your cup first so you can better support others.

If you're frequently finding yourself stuck in a funk, I have some good news. There are several practices that, when performed regularly, will keep you unstuck and moving forward:

- **Meditation.** Practising meditation allows you to stop, breathe, and regain control of your thoughts. When you find your thoughts spiralling and getting away from you, meditation can help bring you back to baseline.
- **Rituals.** Rituals that energise and revitalise you will keep the positive thoughts flowing. It could be exercising in the morning, walking at sunset, or reading before bed

- whatever fills your cup.
- **Motivation.** Motivational videos, podcasts, and quotes can all help shift your state of mind, so have some locked and loaded ready to blast you out of your next funk.
- **Sleep.** Anyone who's ever been sleep-deprived – hello, new parents! – knows that a lack of sleep can seriously bring us down. Are you getting enough sleep to function at your best? If not, it might be time to make some changes.
- **Nutrition.** Research shows that our diets affect our mental health.[12] When in doubt, the key is to consume healthy wholefoods and fewer processed foods. Your body and mind will thank you.
- **Community.** Community is important for our mental health. However, not all communities are created equal. If you want to feel supercharged to succeed, you'll need to surround yourself with the *right* people, people who cheer you on and lift you up. As I learnt over the years, having the wrong people in your circle can be detrimental to your success and wellbeing.

Ask yourself (this can be a tough one), *Do the people closest to me bring out the best in me?* If the people around you aren't supportive, they can end up holding you back. Ultimately, the people you surround yourself with will either uplift and empower you or hinder your growth. Like Tony Robbins said, "The quality of a person's life is most often a direct reflection of the expectations of their peer group." As you spend more time with people, they influence your outlook, which often ends in sharing values, standards, and beliefs.

The key to having a solid community is to surround yourself with people who are your biggest cheerleaders but who also hold you accountable because they want the best for you. For the most part, we can control who we spend our time with, so choose wisely.

Even on the days when you're stuck in a downward spiral and want to give up, it's important to still show up. It's important to keep going. It's the best thing you can do. Yes, make time to meditate, exercise, whatever you need to do for yourself, but that doesn't mean hiding from the world or your problems and letting your business suffer.

> On difficult days, you need to remember
> that you're in control of your thoughts,
> no matter how intrusive they might feel.
> No matter how defeated you feel, keep going.

I like to draw inspiration from the words of Simon Sinek: "Working hard for something we don't care about is called stress: Working hard for something we love is called passion."

Stay strong, approach each day with a warrior's resolve, let your passion be your fuel, and remember that sometimes simply showing up is enough.

INNER WARFARE: AN ACTIVITY TO AWAKEN YOUR WARRIOR

Take Control of Your Mental Dialogue

When the negative mental chatter starts, to get back on track, you first need to figure out what knocked you off the rails. Was it something that happened? Was it something someone said? Or was it a bigger issue you're yet to confront? Determining the trigger not only helps realign your mental dialogue, but it also helps you avoid future negative thought spirals.

Whenever that voice in your head starts trying to tear you down, it's important to recognise it for what it is – complete BS – and take control of the narrative. You're the author of your own story, and you get to decide what you're capable of. Remember, doubt your limits, not your capabilities.

If you do find yourself overcome by negative chatter, here's a simple three-step process you can use to get back on track:

1. **Recognise that your mental dialogue has turned negative.** Before you can change anything, you must first recognise that there's a problem. If you find your mental dialogue shifting into negative territory, stop what you're doing, breathe, and take back control.

2. **Identify the trigger.** When our thoughts spiral, there's usually a trigger. Take time to reflect, journal if necessary, and try to identify what caused that little voice in your head to turn against you. Note the trigger for future reference, and make a plan to avoid the same outcome in the future. We're all about breaking harmful patterns, yeah?
3. **Be your own best friend.** Now it's time to set things right. What is the voice in your head telling you? Is it something you would say to your best friend? Now imagine what you *would* say to your best friend, coming from a place of pure love and respect, about the situation. Be honest. Be real. Make that voice the loudest. That's the one you should be listening to. Figure out exactly what you need to do to get back into a positive headspace, and do it.

Don't let your ego hold you back with negative self-talk. When pursuing your goals, at the very least, you want yourself in your corner. Why let a negative naysayer run amok in your head when you could instead have an avid supporter? It's time to take back your power, be the boss of your thoughts and emotions, and become your own biggest cheerleader. If you need a little extra cheering on, I'm here for you too. You've got this.

A WARRIOR IS FORGED IN BATTLE

At this point in my life, I can honestly say I have no regrets. Yes, I went through some tough times that I would have preferred to avoid at the time, but those challenging situations made me the strong, successful, confident woman I am today. A true warrior isn't made in times of peace and comfort. It's the battles, the adversity, overcoming challenges that develop our strength and resilience.

When I say I don't have any regrets, what I mean is that I'm very aligned with where I'm going in life. I don't get stuck in the past, letting the negative mental chatter hold me back. I don't get rattled by life so much anymore. Instead, I rattle life.

As in business, in life you need a clear plan to get from point A to point B. You need to know where you're going and how you're going to get there. When you have a clear plan that includes what you want, why you want it, and how you're going to get it, it's easier to silence the voice of doubt when it appears. As your own best friend, you'll know whether that sneaky little voice is speaking the truth or not. Sometimes you may actually be on the wrong track. Is the self-doubt there for a reason? Is this something you really want? Is there a better way forward? It's not about ignoring every critical thought that enters your consciousness. It's about examining each one from a place of love and friendship. In doing so, you'll either realise you're on the wrong track or you're doing exactly what you need to do, giving you even more strength and determination to continue down that path.

Master Your Mental Dialogue

1. Be your own best friend, your biggest cheerleader. When the negative mental chatter starts, ask yourself, *What would I say to my best friend in this situation?* You want to be honest with yourself, but you should also be your biggest supporter. Why shouldn't you be your own biggest cheerleader? You absolutely should.

2. Maintaining mastery of your mental dialogue requires constant care. Just because you've tamed the voice in your head for now, don't assume it will last. Be vigilant. The negative self-talk can reappear at any time, and you must be ready to face and thwart it when it does.

3. Always look for the light. Where there's darkness, light isn't far away. When you're experiencing your darkest moments, always remember to look for the light.

4. Doubt your limits, not your capabilities. So many of us are capable of much more than we think, but we doubt our capabilities, so we never get to fully explore them.

5. Money equals choice. Money is only as evil as the person holding it. If you so choose, you can use your wealth in a positive way, creating an impact in the world and building your dream life.

Seek to understand
where that trauma has
come from, heal from
it, and never pass it on.

AWAKENING THE WARRIOR

6

RECONCILE WITH YOUR INNER CHILD

DON'T LET YOUR INNER CHILD RUN THE SHOW

We've discussed harmful patterns, playing the blame game, difficult lessons, and negative self-talk… but where do these seemingly detrimental aspects of our personalities come from? Some, if not many, may stem from childhood. We learn the dance of life from others, and sometimes those people are unqualified to teach it. Whether we want it to or not, our environment shapes our reality. For me, it was definitely the case.

If you were hurt or neglected as a child, you can carry that trauma into adulthood. When my dad left, I was hurt. I felt abandoned, and I later looked for love in all the wrong places. It took me years to realise where my pain was coming from, and it wasn't until our fertility journey that I was able to reconcile with my inner child and heal that relationship with my younger self.

For years, I let my inner child run the show. I let her thoughts, her emotions, her unresolved pain influence my actions. Not exactly ideal in the adult world. However, through self-development and psychedelics, I was able to identify the stories I was telling myself about the world, the ones I unconsciously learnt during childhood, and change them.

If I was going to be a mother, I couldn't let my inner child call the shots. It was time to take back control. Yes, the inner child will always be there, but she shouldn't be in charge. Before I was able to fall pregnant, I had to step into the adult version of myself. Kevin and I both had to drop the stories we were telling ourselves and mature as adults. How could I welcome a baby into the world when my wounded inner child was in control? Children need a certain level of maturity from their parents, mentally, physically, emotionally, and if you haven't reconciled with your inner child, you might not be ready to raise and nurture another.

Once I did the inner work, I felt my inner child grow and mature. Sure, she still has her moments, especially when Kevin and I are arguing, but it's rare nowadays. We try to approach everything from an adult perspective, and we don't get triggered as much by our inner wounds. Honestly, I don't think we ever fully heal from those wounds. We just learn to use them as superpowers.

> *"The purpose of pain is to move us into action not to make us suffer."*
> – *Tony Robbins*

LOOKING FOR LOVE IN ALL THE WRONG PLACES

Before Dad left, he had been a superstar in my eyes. Oh, how quickly that changed. When he left, I didn't understand why. *Am I not worthy? Does he not love me? If he can leave so easily, who's ever going to stay?* When your own father abandons you, abandonment issues are practically unavoidable.

Due to feeling unworthy, I searched for love and validation in all the wrong places. I valued the opinions of others when their opinions didn't matter and mostly brought me down. Still, I didn't fit in. I felt rejected. I was repeating the same pattern again and again, with my inner child running the show.

Due to unmet needs as a child, I experienced relationship issues. It took me a while to recognise the pattern. It took even longer to stop blaming my dad and accept the lesson. *What's the root of the issue? What needs to be healed? How can I reconcile with my inner child?* If you ignore the screams of your inner child, they'll keep getting louder and louder. You must learn the lesson. Whatever trauma is in your past, you must overcome it and heal your relationship with your inner child. Otherwise, you'll keep repeating the same harmful patterns, and the pain and suffering will only get worse.

Personally, I found myself attracted to men who were emotionally unavailable. The problem was, I was searching for love outside of myself because I didn't have my needs met as a child. I didn't get the love I needed from my dad. By seeking out men who were emotionally unavailable, I was mirroring the fact that my dad was emotionally unavailable to me as a child. My choice in men was totally influenced by my abandonment issues. No wonder those relationships failed.

It wasn't until I did psychedelics that I realised my inner child was in control and I needed to heal that relationship. Going into that psychedelic session, I didn't know how I felt about Kevin. I didn't know if we were compatible partners for the dance of life, and I quickly realised that my love for him was conditional, not unconditional, something I learnt from my dad. I loved my furbaby Coco unconditionally, but for some reason I couldn't do the same for Kevin. There was pain in the way. There was a hurt inner child who hadn't learnt to love herself. How could I love another human unconditionally when I couldn't even love myself? Clearly, there was another lesson to accept and a pattern to break.

Through psychedelics, I saw how everything and everyone are connected, and I understood what true unconditional love meant. I became the observer of my own life, and I saw how all the pieces fit together. I saw where all the disconnections were and how to connect them. I had been taught one version of love from my dad, and that was the one that stuck with me, but now I understood another. All the little things I had spent so much time and energy worrying about – they were insignificant in the scheme of infinity.

If I could sit down with my inner child as if I were her mother, ask her, "What's going on with you?" and really try to understand, we could begin to heal our relationship, along with all the others in my life. It was time to reconcile with my inner child, learn to love in a better way, and start living life on my terms.

STOP PLAYING THE VICTIM AND RECLAIM YOUR POWER

Healing my relationship with my inner child healed my relationship with my dad. When my parents split and Dad moved back to Germany, my childhood was predominantly with Mum and my siblings. Even though she put us in therapy early, I struggled to deal with it, and I don't think my emotions evolved enough as a child and teenager. Essentially, my inner child was in control.

As you know, if you want to be successful and content in life, you need to be your own best friend. Growing up in Ireland, loving myself was difficult. Unfortunately, in my home town, many people seemed to hate themselves, and I was on the receiving end of a lot of jealousy. I was modelling, dancing, performing in musicals, and I was often in the local newspaper. Due to the attention I received, certain people would try to bring me down. They thought I had a big ego. "Sonja loves herself," they would say – and not in a positive way. To them, loving yourself was a crime, and people like me who stood too tall had to be cut down to size.

Throughout school, the bullying was intense. I don't think the girls who bullied me even realised they were acting from a place of jealousy. They just saw me excelling and decided I needed to be humbled. But their words weren't humbling. They hurt. They implied that being successful was wrong. They often taunted me with deeply personal insults and even threatened physical violence, waiting at the school gate to beat me for reasons I never knew. Just being me made me a target.

Although the bullying hurt, I didn't allow it to hold me back. Instead, I continued to excel at everything I put my mind to, and it worked out pretty well for me in the end.

Because self-love was practically a criminal act in my home

town, during this time, I wasn't my own best friend at all. In fact, I was far from it. I was an anxious kid, insecure, which all traced back to Dad leaving. I felt unworthy, and my self-esteem plummeted. As I got older, my anxiety and insecurity manifested in control-freak tendencies. I would try to control every situation, as it made me feel safe. Early in our relationship, Kevin and I would often bash heads because I needed to be in control of my environment. It was a masculine response that contradicted my feminine energy. Because we were both bringing predominantly masculine energy to the relationship, we continued to clash until I took steps to heal my relationship with my dad and inner child. I think I got that dominant, masculine, alpha-female energy from my mum, because she had to be both mother and father to us.

For years, I blamed everything that went wrong in my life on my dad. *He's the reason why my life is so messed up*, I'd tell myself. I was stuck in the victim mentality, which left me powerless to move forward. How could I fix the problem when others were to blame? Accepting responsibility for your problems isn't about taking the blame; it's about reclaiming your power to solve them. The warrior's way is to take charge of the situation and not let life lead her about. That doesn't mean you can control everything – you can't – but, to paraphrase an old saying, while you can't control the wind, you can adjust your sails. You have the power to choose the direction in which you head.

To heal my relationship with my dad, I realised I needed to take myself out of the equation and try to understand where he had come from. As it turned out, there was intergenerational trauma involved.

INTERGENERATIONAL TRAUMA – A HAND-ME-DOWN FORGED IN TIMES OF WAR

Dad was the product of wartimes. Both of my grandparents got caught up in World War II. My grandfather was a Nazi soldier, and my grandmother lost both her parents in the war, and almost lost her own life too.

My grandmother got lost during the war and ended up staying in a room with several Jewish women, some of whom were pregnant. She was the youngest among them, the only child in the room, around 13 years old. The Nazis were looking for them, and there was nowhere to run. Right before the soldiers arrived, the women wrapped my grandmother in an old carpet, hoping to keep her hidden, safe, and alive. Thanks to the quick thinking of those Jewish women, my grandmother survived. The others weren't so lucky. I can only imagine the trauma she must have suffered, losing her parents, almost losing her own life, and witnessing those who helped her shot and killed right there in that room. How does anyone move on from that?

Eventually, she met my grandfather, who was still a Nazi soldier. For him, it was kill or be killed. There were no other options. Once I understood what my grandparents had experienced, suddenly I saw my dad as his full self. Being raised by two parents who were traumatised by war, there was no way he could possibly have his shit together. When he became a father, he didn't know what it meant to love a child because he didn't get the right type of love from his parents. He then inadvertently handed his trauma down to me. Even the most hardened warriors must bear the scars of war.

For my grandparents, after everything they had been through, Dad was the only source of happiness in their lives, and they put him on a pedestal. In their eyes, he could do no wrong, which was why he didn't see anything wrong with leaving us. He was used to getting his way and doing what he wanted, with emotion removed from the equation.

My mistake was expecting Dad to be the man I wanted him to be, not the man he was, which was never going to serve me in life. By doing the inner work, I learnt to accept him for who he was and find the positives in all the struggles of my childhood. If he hadn't left us when he did, I wouldn't have witnessed my mother's unwavering strength and resilience raising three kids on her own. Without those tough times, I wouldn't be the warrior I am today.

As a hopeful mother-to-be, the last thing I wanted to do was hand that same trauma down to my child. I couldn't allow myself to carry it through pregnancy and into motherhood. It was up to me to break the chain of intergenerational trauma, lead with my heart, and pave a new way forward. The world needs more light, not more darkness, and the last thing we want is to be passing our demons on to our children. One of the biggest motivations for turning my life around was wanting to one day be a mum I could be proud of. All the pain I went through as a child made me realise that I didn't want my children to ever experience that. To accomplish this, I had to heal my inner child, build resilience, and lead from a place of love. I had to be the mum my child needed me to be.

I now have a much better relationship with my dad. He's a part of my life, but I have no expectations of him. He is who he is, and I've learnt to accept that.

When it comes to me and my business, he's one of my biggest supporters. He's proud of what I've accomplished. I don't need that from him now, although I would have liked to have had it as a child. Because *I'm* proud of what I've accomplished, I don't need it from anyone else. I'm my own biggest supporter and cheerleader now, and it's all I really need. Anything else is just a bonus.

Since healing the relationship with my dad, I was also able to heal the relationship with my hurt inner child, and life got so much better. Suddenly, everything started to happen for me; everything started to flow, which was a nice change.

Honestly, there was a point where I never thought I'd be able to overcome the pain of Dad leaving. I never thought I'd be able to forgive him. I never thought we'd have a meaningful relationship again. Being a warrior isn't just about fighting at every turn. It's also about knowing when to surrender, when to forgive, and when to find a peaceful way forward. Sometimes the path of surrender and acceptance requires the most strength.

FINDING LOVE IN ALL THE RIGHT PLACES

When I look back at my life, I see all the people I was infatuated with. I put them on a pedestal because I thought they were on a completely different level to me. I believed they had something I didn't, some magical quality that made them special. While many of them did have skills I didn't have, below the surface we weren't so different. Once I got to know them, I realised they weren't so different from me after all. Deep down, we're all very much the same. However, because I suffered from low self-esteem, I frequently felt inferior, like I was somehow less than the people around me.

We often think we see something special in people, something we believe we don't have and may never have, and we admire them for it. What we don't realise is that the reason we admire it is because it's in us too. We just don't see it. The trick is to stop looking outwardly and start looking inwardly. Instead of directing your admiration at others, you can turn it on yourself, building a genuine sense of self-worth.

For so long, I was outwardly influenced by the people and world around me. I kept looking for answers externally. I'd go from coach to coach, saying, "Give me the answers. Tell me what I need to do." While those coaches could guide me to answers, they couldn't give them to me. To get them, I had to look within. If I wanted to be successful in business, an amazing wife, and eventually a mum, I had to look inward and nurture that relationship with myself and my inner child. From that, everything else would flow – and it did.

The moment I made peace with who I am, loving myself unconditionally on a spiritual and emotional level, everything changed. I started attracting the most amazing clients; money flowed freely, and success came easily. Of course, I still had to work hard in my business, but everything just *flowed*.

A word of warning – when you're growing, you must remain humble. Don't assume you know better than anyone else. Ego can be the death of success. Even though I run a successful business, I still think of myself as a regularl person. You shouldn't be putting anyone on a pedestal, including yourself. You can know you're worthy of success and still be humble at the same time.

When I looked inward and reconciled with my inner child, all of my relationships improved. I was able to put myself in my dad's shoes and see love in places where I'd been adamant it didn't exist. Where I expected to find more pain, I instead found love. In my marriage, I was able to let go and stop trying to be the man in the relationship. Surprise, surprise – it's difficult to fall pregnant when you're full of masculine energy.

It took a lot of work and reflection, but I finally got it together and arrived at a place where I had a good relationship with myself. I was about to bring a baby into the world – a blank canvas – and she would reflect back all the parts of myself I didn't like. Before I could be a mother, I had to put all the traumatic events of my past to bed. I couldn't have them affecting my relationship with my daughter. I couldn't pass that trauma on to her.

When I first started down the path of self-development and

self-discovery, I didn't realise how many things were blocking me from finding true success in life and becoming a mum. I'm so proud of how far Kevin and I have come, working through so much to get where we are today. We were both living in our own worlds of pain, but now we're in a much better place. Yeah, it took us a while, but it's now clearer than ever that we were meant to be together.

INNER WARFARE: AN ACTIVITY TO AWAKEN YOUR WARRIOR

Healing and Reconciliation

To reconcile with my inner child, I had to identify the positives in past experiences that I had labelled negative. Yeah, not always easy, but let's give it a go. I know that digging up the past can be traumatic, but burying it is much worse in the long run. I learnt that lesson the hard way. So, I want you to think back to the most challenging events of your past, the ones that may be straining the relationship between you and your inner child or past self. **Write them down.** Next – and this is the liberating part – I want you to identify the positive outcomes of each event. **Write them down**. There *is* a positive in every situation. Some are just easier to see than others.

For example, by the time I was a teenager, I was rebelling due to Dad leaving, and it may have looked like I was totally messing up my life. To some extent, I probably was, but, at the same time, I learnt street smarts, how to read people, and how to look out for myself, all valuable life skills that not everyone learns. My teenage years were tough but if I'd had a different experience, I wouldn't be the resilient warrior I am today, a huge positive. So, under **challenging event**, I'd write: *Difficult (or should I say wild) teenage years due to Dad leaving*, and under **positive outcome**, I'd write: *Learning street smarts*. See? There's a positive in everything. Now it's your turn.

Challenging Event	Positive Outcome
....	....
....	....
....	....
....	....
....	....
....	....
....	....
....	....
....	....

Challenging Event	Positive Outcome

By identifying the positives in your most difficult moments, they become fuel that propels you forward instead of shackles that hold you in place. I know that reconciling with the past isn't as simple as writing a list, but it's a great place to start. Remember, we're all works in progress, and there will always be more inner work to do.

Reconcile with Your Inner Child

1. Don't let your inner child run the show. When you make decisions or take action, is it the wise adult in control? Or the hurt inner child? Just like your young kids shouldn't be running the household, your inner child should never be running the show.

2. Try to understand your hurt inner child. If you feel that your inner child is in pain, the first step is to understand why. *What's going on with you?* is a great question to start with. From there, you can begin to peel back the layers, identify root causes, and begin the reconciliation process.

3. Break the cycle of intergenerational trauma. Trauma is like a virus that can be passed down through generations. The cure? Seek to understand where that trauma has come from, heal from it, and never pass it on to others. You can choose to break the cycle.

4. Sometimes acceptance requires the most strength. While sometimes we must fight, struggle, and resist to better our situations, other times we must make peace with where we are and where we've come from. You can't change the past, but you sure as hell can learn from it. Often, accepting the past for what it is and people for who they are requires the most strength and courage.

5. Identify the positives in past struggles. A powerful step towards accepting the past and healing your inner child is identifying the positives in each challenge. With every minus, there is a plus; it's the law of the universe. You simply must be willing to see it.

This is Saige as an embryo before she was implanted.

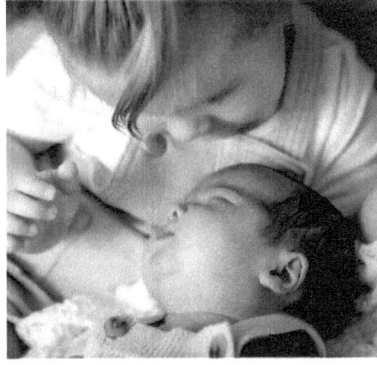

Setting boundaries is
an act of self-love.

AWAKENING THE WARRIOR

7

SET IMPENETRABLE BOUNDARIES

BOUNDARIES, BOUNDARIES, AND MORE BOUNDARIES

Growing up, Mum always talked about boundaries. She talked about them so much we were practically allergic to the word. While she may have sounded like a broken record, she was absolutely onto something.

In a house full of girls, setting boundaries was difficult. We would constantly borrow each other's stuff without asking. It was a normal part of life. I also didn't set firm boundaries with my friends, mainly because, no matter how much mum tried to teach me, I didn't fully understand the nature of boundaries. Now I have a much better understanding.

Essentially, boundaries are about ring-fencing your time and energy and only letting in those who deserve it. To maintain those boundaries, you must learn when and how to say 'no'. It's a powerful word. If something doesn't serve you, in business and in life, it's important to speak your mind and not spend energy where it would be wasted. That energy is best conserved for the parts where it will have the most impact.

In my teenage years especially, I was a bit of a people pleaser, constantly trying to fit in, and I always landed on my arse. I wasn't listening to my intuition. By listening to your gut, you'll get a good idea of where your boundaries should be.

For example, I've outgrown some friends over the years. Basically, we went down different paths, and, in the end, we were simply vibrating at different frequencies. We became mismatched. As I moved forward with my life, I set some firm boundaries.

There were no arguments or tough conversations; I just wasn't as available, and we moved apart organically. Different frequencies.

Enforcing your boundaries doesn't mean constantly confronting and arguing with people. At least, it doesn't have to. It's about speaking up and being honest with people. You don't need to be aggressive, just calm, clear, and firm. Ultimately, it's on you to ensure that your boundaries are clear and to clarify when needed. Sure, when you start speaking up for yourself, some people might be put off at first, but most people respect someone who respects themselves, and having boundaries is one of the most loving and respectful things you can do for yourself.

> *"Daring to set boundaries is about having the courage to love ourselves, even when we risk disappointing others."*
> – Brené Brown

Yes, many of us experience fear and anxiety around confrontation, speaking our truths, and setting boundaries – I know I did – but the more you do it, the easier it gets, especially when you begin to see the benefits. It's temporary discomfort for long-term gain. While it may be difficult to push through, it's nothing compared to the consequences of letting a molehill of a problem gradually turn into a mountain. Been there. Done that. It never ends well. You're much better off setting firm boundaries from the start.

LAYING SOLID FOUNDATIONS FOR MOTHERHOOD

When I was pregnant with Saige, there were people telling me to slow down, take it easy, don't do too much. I tried to explain my situation, but they couldn't understand that because I love what I do, I don't see it as work, and I felt no need to slow down. They thought I was bonkers, but I was doing the dance I wanted to do. When the baby came, I would get my downtime. Until then, my energy was best spent setting up my business to thrive while I was gone. I didn't want to get dragged back to work early when I had a newborn who needed me. I had to set some firm boundaries, but, in order for them to hold, I also had to lay the groundwork.

My biggest why in life was to create a business around my kids. I knew what it was like to have parents who weren't present, or couldn't be as present as they would have liked, and I wanted my kids to have a different experience. While I was addicted to the success of my business, more than anything I wanted to be a mum – and a great one at that. To be able to step away from your business, you need a solid team to steer the ship while you're gone. You need people you can rely on.

When I first set up my business, I didn't plan to expand. I never thought I'd be hiring a team. However, with success came organic growth. My first hire was my Google Ads and SEO specialist. I was still in charge of strategy and results, but now I had someone working in the background so I didn't have to do absolutely everything, which opened up my time to help more clients.

From there, the team expanded, and I hired only people I had worked with previously and were incredible at their jobs.

I'll admit, in the lead-up to my due date, I had a moment of panic. *Fuck*, I thought. *I'm having a baby in five weeks' time, and I've got to hand my whole business over to my team. But I can't. No one's going to do it like I do. It just won't work.* I took some deep breaths, calmed myself down, and realised that a lack of sleep from pregnancy insomnia might have been making me a little irrational. I had already learnt the lesson about not trying to control everything, and I didn't need to repeat it. One thing I couldn't control was childbirth. I had no idea when my daughter was coming, just a rough due date, and it stressed me out. I guess I still had some work to do on my control-freak tendencies.

When trying to reduce reliance on yourself in your business, the key is to examine all the tasks you do and see what you can outsource or delegate. If your team is competent and happy, and your clients are well looked after, your business will function without you. Are you struggling to delegate? Been there. It's just your ego asserting that you must do everything yourself – only you can do it! – but it's not true. Your ego wants you to feel significant but if you can't let go, learn to delegate, and find significance elsewhere, you'll take the hit later down the track. If I didn't learn to put faith in my team, I wouldn't have been able to confidently step away from my business when the baby came. Either the business would have crumbled while I couldn't work at full capacity, or I would've jumped right back into the pilot's seat, spending very little quality time with my newborn child. To me, none of those options were acceptable, so I learnt to let go and trust in the team I had built.

When building my team, I focused on hiring highly skilled people who don't just pigeonhole themselves into one specific duty. What makes me so happy as an employer is seeing my team take the initiative and put themselves in my shoes or the shoes of our clients, as it lightens the mental load that naturally comes with owning a business. Taking the initiative is an innate skill, and unfortunately not everyone possesses it. My team may come with a high price tag, but each person can wear multiple hats, saving resources in the long run. If I had hired only juniors when we first started growing, there's no way I would have been able to step back and let the team take over when the baby came. Fortunately, I had a powerful team behind me that really stepped up – and continues to step up – when I need them.

SHARED VALUES AND THE POWER OF PENGUINS

As my business grew, one key to its continued success was surrounding myself with a team with shared values. They care about the business as much as I do. Exactly what you want in a team, right? We treat one another like family, and we have a relationship of mutual trust, respect, loyalty, and integrity, which helps me sleep at night.

Look, you don't have to be everyone's cup of tea. If someone doesn't vibe with you or you don't vibe with them, it's okay. It's a part of being human, but we sometimes forget it, feeling like we need to connect with everyone. When building my team, I chose people who I did vibe with and who shared my values. Each member of The Search Republic team not only shares my values but also understands why they're important. They know that I won't take on a client who doesn't align with our values. Coming from other agencies where it wouldn't even be a consideration, it's a welcome change. They know I'm not all about the money. I'm more about finding the right fit and building relationships based on trust, respect, loyalty, and integrity. I'd never sacrifice my values for short-term gain, and my team knows this.

I also make sure that, at every opportunity, I tell them how great they are. If I'd had an appreciative boss, maybe I wouldn't have felt the need to go out on my own. In that sense, I'm glad I had those unpleasant experiences. I wouldn't be where I am today without them. See, a positive in everything.

As well as building my team up emotionally, I try to mentor them as much as possible, building them up with the skills and tools to navigate life. I learnt many lessons the hard way, but that doesn't mean they should too. It doesn't mean *you* should either. If my mentorship or this book can show someone a smoother path to success, then it's worth its weight in gold.

When I rebranded my business as The Search Republic in 2022, I chose penguins to represent our brand identity. Why? Because penguins mate for life. It's a trait that reflects my passion for long-term client relationships. Through my business identity, I wanted to represent the genuine lifelong partnerships we offer clients and how we walk every step of the path to growth with them.

Penguins select a pebble to 'propose' a partnership, which is the perfect symbolism for my belief in providing valuable Google Ads and SEO insights before expecting a commitment from clients. In penguin partnerships, both parents work together to care for their young, a devotion to teamwork that parallels my collaboration with clients for ongoing improvement.

There's also a spiritual component to me choosing penguins. They aren't afraid to go through uncomfortable territory in pursuit of their dreams. They can literally work and survive in the most challenging environments, which aligns with my warrior spirit.

As part of our launch strategy, we adopted two penguins, Penny and Bobby, through the WWF. Penguins mate for life, and I can't help but admire their loyalty.

AUDITING YOUR ENERGY – TOUGH DECISION TIME

Friendship wise, we intuitively know the people who are meant to be in our lives. They stand out by offering an equal energy exchange. For example, if you feel like you're the one who has to maintain the friendship without getting anything back in return, it's a sure sign that there's a mismatch. In every good relationship, you should feel like an equal in every way.

When determining where to set boundaries, you should first

audit your focus and the people and tasks demanding your time and energy.

Firstly, let's talk about focus. It's important to audit where you're spending your time. Is it serving you? Or is it distracting you from your goals? We can get so caught up in serving others that we neglect our own priorities and needs. Or we're too busy watching what others are doing to focus on ourselves or our own businesses. Once you start comparing yourself to others, especially to what you see on social media, you can begin to lose sight of your own accomplishments. If you're comparing yourself to others, stop. Stay in your own lane. Remember what's unique about you and what you do. You don't need to mimic anyone else. In fact, it will only stop you from reaching your full potential.

Secondly, let's talk about the people you surround yourself with. Do they make you feel good about yourself? The people you're sharing an equal energy exchange with, keep them in your circle. The others? It might be time to do some house cleaning. Anyone who's not allowing you to be your true authentic self, you may need to distance yourself from. That doesn't mean they can't remain acquaintances but if you keep them in your close circle, they'll likely do more harm than good in the long run. Sure, you don't want to hurt anyone's feelings, but it's much better to deal with the temporary discomfort of ending a taxing friendship than the long-term consequences of ignoring the problem.

As I got busier and busier, I needed to better prioritise where I spent my time, and I couldn't give my friends as much attention as before. Some were able to respect that, and some weren't.

I'm a firm believer that if people can't respect your boundaries, they aren't meant to be long-term friends anyway. They're simply playing a guest spot in the series of your life. They're not a permanent cast member.

I'll offer some blunt advice: **if the people in your circle don't clap the loudest when you succeed, get a new circle.**

It's one of my biggest mottos in life. If the people around you are trying to cut you down, compete with you, or take from you, they aren't the people who should be around you. Period. Jealousy and envy don't serve anyone. I'm all about 'friend cleanses' when necessary. It may sound harsh, and it may be tough to do, especially when people have been in your life for years or even decades, but life is short. Wouldn't you rather spend it with the people who will cheer for you the loudest?

INNER WARFARE: AN ACTIVITY TO AWAKEN YOUR WARRIOR

Time, Energy, and Focus Audit

It's time to audit your focus and the people around you. Scary, I know, but trust me – it's for your own good. Firstly, I want you to consider all the people and tasks that are demanding your time, energy, and focus. **Write them down**. Next, I want you to determine whether there's an equal energy exchange. Are you getting out as much as you put in, yes or no? **Write it down.**

For example, in the past, I realised that participating in too many group chats was seriously stealing my time, draining my energy, and shifting my focus away from more important tasks. Sound familiar? I already spend enough time on social media for my business, and being in so many group chats wasn't serving me at all. Who wants 20 or more group chats screaming for their attention all throughout the day? Not me. I simply have too much on my plate. So, for **task or person**, I'd write: *Participating in pointless group chats.* For **equal energy exchange**, I'd write: *No.* It's not that I don't want to keep in touch with the people involved, but it's not something I can continue to invest time and energy in. The people who matter will stay in our lives regardless.

Task or Person	Equal Energy Exchange
....	....
....	....
....	....
....	....
....	....
....	....

Task or Person	Equal Energy Exchange
....	....
....	....
....	....
....	....
....	....
....	....
....	....
....	....
....	....
....	....
....	....
....	....
....	....
....	....

You may have guessed it – now that you've identified areas where investing your time, energy, and focus isn't serving you, it's time to set some firm boundaries. You've got this.

TAKE CONTROL OF YOUR ATTENTION

If you're someone who has trouble redirecting their energy, I want to give you a little extra advice to help you channel your attention in a more productive direction. Sometimes we can get so wrapped up and stressed in areas of our lives and businesses that don't serve our wider vision. We're putting precious time and energy into tasks or thoughts that don't move us closer to our goals, dancing to the wrong beat, often without even realising it.

Many years ago, I made the conscious decision to not allow myself to be consumed by the sensationalism of the media. However, during the COVID-19 pandemic, I and many other businesses were put on the back foot, filled with uncertainty and terrified we could lose everything we had worked so hard to build. Due to the unprecedentedness of the situation and the high stakes involved, I had no choice but to pay attention to the news to stay up to date. The whole experience reaffirmed my earlier decision to avoid giving the media my valuable attention.

Quickly, I became anxious, and I lost a lot of sleep. It wasn't just the threat of losing my business, although it was a factor. Constantly being tuned in to the news fuelled my fear and anxiety. I was at war with an enemy that didn't exist, which took me away from the real battle – ensuring my business survived the pandemic. I wasn't protecting myself. I wasn't guarding my mind, and it showed in the shift in my mental dialogue to a more fearful, anxious, and pessimistic voice. I know many people who went through the pandemic experienced a similar shift.

As Tony Robbins said, "Energy flows where attention goes," and my attention was more focused on the sensationalist media than on pushing forward with my goals. It didn't matter that we were experiencing a once-in-a-lifetime pandemic. Putting so much focus on the news wasn't serving me or my business. Yes, there were certain things we all needed to know, such as current restrictions and health advice, but we didn't need to know everything. At a certain point, it wasn't the pandemic that put the brakes on me and my business; it was my perception of it and the distraction of the media. Clearly, it was time to redirect my energy in a more positive direction and regain control of the narrative in my head.

Are there areas in your life you need to shift your energy away from? Here's what worked for me:

1. **What's something I want to accomplish in the next 3 years?** Ask yourself this question to point yourself in a more positive direction. By focusing on your goals for the next 3 years, you can shift your focus away from whatever negative thoughts are draining your energy now.
2. **Why is it important to me?** Knowing what you want to accomplish is great, but it's important to know *why* you want to accomplish it. By reflecting on why you want something, you'll either reinforce your decision to pursue it or identify when your reasons are lacking.

3. **What can I do right now to get closer to that goal?**
   This is a big one. If your energy is being hijacked by an unproductive task or thought pattern, identifying actions you can take right now to move towards a conscious objective forces you to redirect your focus.
4. **Set intermittent goals to help you along the way.**
   All lofty goals and long journeys require a series of steps to complete. It's not just a matter of going from A to B. So, set yourself monthly, quarterly, half-yearly goals – whatever suits the situation – to ensure that you always know you're moving towards the next important milestone. Oh, and don't forget to hold yourself accountable.

Once I switched my focus to a major goal, I no longer felt the media circus around the pandemic demanding my attention. It just didn't seem important anymore because I had a roadmap to move me forward and milestones to reach.

The key is to first understand what's draining your energy for little to no return on investment. I know that it can be hard to take back control when something has you under its spell, like the news captured me. However, if you can find something more compelling to direct your focus at, such as growing your business, mastering a new skill, or creating something great, the energy black hole in your life will lose its pull.

LET'S TALK BUSINESS BOUNDARIES

When it comes to my clients, I'm very clear on expectations right from the start so they know exactly what to expect within a certain timeframe. In our first meeting, I explain precisely what they can expect in terms of work and results month by month. The communication lines are always open, and I'm constantly in contact with clients to manage expectations, maintain transparency, and keep them up-to-date. I've found that the more we communicate about what we're working on, the less likely clients are to cause problems and disrupt the process. Results don't happen overnight, and keeping people in the loop helps them maintain patience and see the value in what we're doing. Sometimes, however, clients do cross the line.

One particular client just couldn't keep his hands off his Google Ads campaign, no matter how firmly I warned him to leave it alone. He was a bit of a control freak and wanted to tweak the campaign himself. Big mistake. Gradually, I noticed a drop in the results. The campaign had been well-designed, so there was no good reason for the drop-off. On further investigation, I noticed that the client had added some keywords, changed the bidding strategy, the targeting, and the ad copy, which may seem innocent enough, but it had clearly had a negative effect on the results.

With this specific client, I knew a phone conversation wouldn't do the trick. I needed to have a frank and honest conversation with him face to face, or screen to screen, so I arranged a video call. "Come on, buddy, stop touching your Google Ads campaign. I warned you at the start, and now we've seen a drop in results. Is that what you want? I don't step on your toes in your business, so I don't expect you to step on mine. If you want to do it yourself, go for it. I can't have you sabotaging our work. If you keep it up, I'll have to fire you. Do you understand?"

"Okay, fine, I promise I won't touch it anymore." And he never did.

Essentially, I set clear boundaries with every client. If they repeatedly cross those boundaries, I'm not afraid to have the tough conversations, which usually go something like this. "Look, I was clear on expectations from the start. The way you want to operate won't get the results you want, and it's also costing us more time and resources than it's worth. I don't think we're the right fit." Then I end their contract and let them take their business elsewhere.

Parting ways with clients isn't something I take lightly, and it's not something I like to do, but sometimes, for my own wellbeing, the wellbeing of my team and the wellbeing of my business, it must be done for various reasons. For example, once the contracts are signed, some clients want to treat me like an employee, like I work for them and must bend to their every demand, but that's not why I got into business. I'm here to get results, and I have no time or tolerance for nonsense. I'm a straight shooter. I tell it like it is. If a client is being disrespectful and crossing my boundaries, I'll address the issue and try to resolve it. I know that some people see confrontation as negative, but I believe in confronting problems head-on. If you don't address the elephant in the room, it keeps growing bigger, and bigger, and bigger, until it becomes completely unmanageable. If I let these types of problems snowball, I would be ignoring the past lesson about speaking my truth before a difficult situation gets even worse. If you don't give yourself the option to fire clients, you're setting yourself up to get trapped in an arrangement that not only benefits no one but is likely damaging to your business and your mental health.

Look, I know that when you're first starting out in business, you may not have the freedom and cash flow to reject or fire every incompatible client. However, if they don't align with your values and are putting an unnecessary drain on your time and resources, is it really worth the effort when your energy could be better spent elsewhere? It's all about setting high standards for yourself, your business, and your clients.

To help filter out incompatible clients, I apply my values of trust, respect, loyalty, and integrity. If someone doesn't demonstrate all four, "Sorry, I don't think we're the right fit." It's as simple as that. In the past, I've accepted clients that held only two or three of my values, and it backfired every time. Lesson learnt.

If a client or anyone in your life is demanding excessive time and energy, it might be time for a tough conversation to create some distance or cut them loose altogether. Whatever you do, know this: you don't need to take anyone's shit.

SET FIRM BOUNDARIES BETWEEN WORK AND HOME

Some boundaries don't need to be set with confrontation and tough conversations. Some of the boundaries you may need to set are to protect you from yourself, especially if you're a workaholic. While putting all your available time and energy into your business or career isn't necessarily a bad thing, we all need to disconnect from the grind occasionally if we want to avoid overwork and burnout.

To separate work and home life, I've taken my work email off my phone completely. In 2023, I was experiencing adrenal fatigue, and constantly being connected to my business via my phone was a big contributor. Before setting that boundary, I'd wake up in the morning and check my emails before I even got out of bed, starting every day the wrong way. I hadn't even properly woken up, and I was already stressed. When I'm at my desk, I'm in a much better headspace to deal with work. I'm in the zone. Lying in bed, still half asleep… not so much. It's scary because a lot of business owners possess this bad habit and start their day this way.

I've also set a firm boundary for social media. Because my business is online and social media is a big part of that, the boundary can get a little blurry. To help clarify the line, I switch my phone off at 6 pm every night and don't turn it back on again until around 7 am each morning, after I've done my meditation, angel cards, and read my mindset book, starting the day on the right foot. If instead I wake up and immediately start scrolling social media, I'm bombarded with chaos before my day has even begun. My brain just isn't ready to deal with it then. Why do I switch my phone off completely? Because if it's still on, I feel the pull, as if it's whispering to me, tempting me back, trying to convince me I'm going to miss something important, which is simply not true. If something urgent does come up when I'm off the grid, people know to call Kevin, so I still have peace of mind that they can reach me when they need to.

When I set this boundary, my sleep and energy improved, and I had more time to focus on the important things, like family. I wanted to be present for my daughters, and I don't want them competing with my phone for attention. When you're with someone and you're scrolling on your phone, it makes them feel like they're second-best and not worthy of your focus. I've been on the receiving end many times, and it feels terrible. Outside of work hours, I'm no longer Sonja The Search Queen; I'm a present wife and mum, which allows quality conversations and connections with my family.

SHOW UP, OWN IT, AND BE REAL

When you set boundaries, you're taking accountability for your part in how you interact with people and the world. People aren't mind readers. If something doesn't sit right with you, it's on you to do something about it.

You're not ever going to be everyone's cup of tea. It's not possible. Some people will like you. Some won't. Some might even despise you, and that's okay. Is it worth losing sleep over? No way. I've said it once, and I'll say it again: people's opinions of you don't pay the bills. Don't let your mental dialogue start creating stories and put you in a negative thought spiral. Creating stories does nothing but waste everyone's time. It's your ego trying to keep you stuck. Don't let it. See, there are stories, and then there's the truth. Being open with people, owning who you are, and setting boundaries when necessary is the best way to ensure you're always living in truth.

During my pregnancies with Saige and Willow, I struggled with insomnia, and there were plenty of mornings when I'd walk into the office sleep-deprived. Before it became an issue, I let everyone know the situation. "Guys, I've hardly had any sleep, so if I'm direct with any of you today, that's why. Please don't take it personally. It's just me hating on life." By pre-empting the potential issue, taking accountability, and explaining the situation, I avoided creating any long-term issues between me and my team. When you do this, you're not just putting your team at ease. You're also ensuring that you're honouring yourself by showing up as your authentic self. You're not changing for anyone.

When I was younger, I always felt like I had to be around people to feel safe and validated, which meant I was constantly seeking out social situations where I couldn't be my true self. I felt like I had to be who the people around me wanted me to be. It was a tough way to live. Once I awakened the warrior within, that completely flipped on its head. **If I can't be myself 100 percent**

at a social gathering, I don't go. When I'm present, you get 250 percent of me. I don't want to put on an act to keep others happy. You get the real raw me, or you get nothing. Simple as that.

SEPARATING SONJA THE SEARCH QUEEN FROM THE SEARCH REPUBLIC AND MASTERING SOCIAL MEDIA

When I chose to put more emphasis on my personal brand, I had to decide what I would present to my audience. Firstly, I wanted to be authentically Sonja. That part was non-negotiable. What people saw online would be what they got when they met me in real life. Being me was the easy part. I also had to decide what type of content I would post. What did my audience want to know? How could I differentiate myself from my business? What type of content would be true to me and my values while helping me stand out in the roaring seas of social media, which threaten to swallow the meek whole, never to be seen nor heard from again?

Through The Search Queen, I was able to show people who I am and what I stand for. Anyone who follows me knows my values and knows they can trust me. I've put myself out there so much that there's very little mystique. What you see is what you get, and my followers have practically seen it all.

Essentially, Sonja The Search Queen is all about putting myself out there and educating people around Google Search as well as motherhood, mindset, fertility, resilience, mumpreneur lifestyle, and balancing business and motherhood, whereas The Search Republic is just about Google Search. In a way, I wanted to separate my personal brand from my business. I didn't want to feel like I was tethered to The Search Republic and it couldn't run without me, especially with a baby on the way. If I needed to step away for long periods, I needed to feel confident that the business could stand on its own legs without The Search Queen holding it up. If I didn't separate myself from the business, I'd have a hard time stepping back.

LIVING YOUR PERSONAL BRAND IS A FULL-TIME JOB

When you're building and maintaining a personal brand, being authentic is even more important. Your online persona should match the real you. You're a fearless warrior, not a shady assassin, and wearing a mask only harms your image in the long run.

Have you ever followed someone online only to meet them and realise they're a completely different person (often for the worse)? It has certainly happened to me. Once you see through the charade, it's impossible to see that person the same again. It's really damaging to their personal brand, especially when they turn out to be not just different but stand-offish in real life.

Sometimes I meet people at events who know me, but I have no idea who they are. Do you think I say so? Of course not. I've been on the receiving end of that one, and it feels terrible. During one encounter, I realised the business coach I had been messaging back and forth with on social media had no idea who I was and likely outsourced her social media engagement to someone else, which would be forgivable… *but* she showed little interest in having a real conversation with me. There was no equal energy exchange.

When I attend an event, I often meet people who follow me on social media, and it's important that I show up authentically so they aren't disappointed when they meet me. Even if I don't know them personally, it doesn't mean I can't be friendly, respectful, and engage them in conversation. Even when I'm offline and out of the office, I'm still my personal brand, and I need to reflect that at all times. Sure, always being 'on' takes effort, but it's well worth it to leave a good impression. I've seen people in business who think they're 'all that', and they're not afraid to hide it. It's not about confidence or self-love either. It's a superiority complex, and often they don't even know the way they're showing up is hurting their brand. They don't understand the importance of connection when it comes to doing business. If someone has a good connection and relationship with you, they're more likely to want to work with you. Nowadays, people don't necessarily want to do business with you because of what you do. They're more focused on who you are. What additional value do you bring to the table? Are you someone people want to be around? Or are you arrogant, rude, and standoffish? Does your online persona match how you show up offline?

Even though I've had a lot of success, I've remained humble.

It's who I am. I don't think I'm better than anyone else. I don't think I'm above them. At the same time, I don't put anyone else on a pedestal. As an awakening warrior, ego and idolisation will only hold you back, whereas humility and respect will propel you forward.

When people know what you stand for and you live up to their expectations, you become more relatable. Perhaps they see themselves in you, or maybe they see the person they want to be. Either way, when you know who you are and what you stand for, people feel that energy. They feel your surety and authenticity, and they can't help but want to be around it.

Set Impenetrable Boundaries

1. Audit your energy. To help identify where you should place your boundaries, perform an energy audit. Are you directing your focus towards people or tasks that aren't serving you? If so, it's time to lay down some firm boundaries.

2. Perform a friend cleanse and fire clients when necessary. If someone in your life, whether it be a friend or client, is making your life unnecessarily hard, it might be time to cut them loose. Think of it as an act of love and respect (towards yourself).

3. Address your problems head-on. When an issue arises and a boundary is required, it's much better to deal with it immediately than to let the problem persist. If you're slow to act, a minor annoyance could turn into a major concern.

4. Set firm boundaries between work and home. Workaholics won't want to hear this, but they're the people who need to hear it most. To ensure you can bring everything to your business or career, you must separate your work and home life. Without a firm boundary in place, it's difficult to know where one ends and the other begins. Avoid burnout at all costs.

5. Your online persona should match the real you. Don't fake it online. If you're pretending to be someone you're not, you're only going to disappoint your audience when they meet the real you. Eventually, the person behind the mask will be revealed. The world is a small place, and people talk.

Only by looking back
do we understand
the growth that
was taking place.

AWAKENING THE WARRIOR

8

SHOW UP AND SURRENDER TO THE EXPERIENCE

MOTHERHOOD INCOMING...

When I was pregnant with Saige, with my due date approaching, I had to prepare to slow down, step back, and let my more-than-capable team take the reins. In the lead-up, I ticked off so many boxes and achieved everything I had set out to do before I had kids. The Search Republic was thriving; we had moved offices twice as we outgrew old premises, and, importantly, the business could run without me. While true mastery takes a lifetime to achieve, I had at least grown competent at the dance of business. I knew most of the steps, perhaps even invented a few of my own, and I put on a great performance. I was unstoppable!

When you build up that sort of momentum, it can be hard to jump off the merry-go-round, and I had to be real about the situation. *You've done the work,* I told myself. *The business will run fine without you. It's time to step back and enjoy being a mum.* Easier said than done, apparently.

As my due date approached, the hormones were hitting hard. *How will I do this? What if the baby comes early? I'm not ready yet.* There were many tears and meltdowns, but in the end I managed to take back control of my mental dialogue. *Okay, so the business is taken care of. Stressing isn't good for the baby. I need to surrender to the experience and trust that the universe has my back.*

The universe only gives us what we can handle, even if it doesn't always seem that way. I had been through tough times before, testing my resilience to the max and almost admitting defeat, but I fought through to the other side every time. Every challenge was an opportunity for growth. If things didn't go according to plan – when do they ever? – I could accept that. As Tony Robbins said, "Life is not happening to you, it's happening for you." Everything in my life up to that point had happened for a reason. Why would the rest of my life be any different? I was ready to surrender to the experience, knowing that the universe would give me exactly what I needed in the end, whatever that might be.

STOP FIGHTING UNWINNABLE BATTLES

What does it mean to surrender to an experience? For much of my life, I always felt like I had to be in control. It made me feel safe. But we can never fully be in control. It's not how the universe works. Fighting against reality is like swimming against a rip in the ocean – you'll only tire yourself out and potentially drown. It's much better to surrender, go with the flow, and conserve your energy for when it's really time to swim.

When I couldn't fall pregnant, I tried to take control of the situation. I did all the research and used every supplement and therapy under the sun. It seemed that the more I tried to make a baby happen, the less likely it seemed I would get what I wanted. Eventually, I learnt a tough lesson: I couldn't change fate, and I had to accept the path the universe was trying to take me down. So, I stepped back, and asked, *What are you trying to show me?* Of course, I still had many obstacles to overcome on my path to pregnancy, but I didn't try to swim against the current. Instead,

I swam with it, acknowledging each tough lesson along the way, knowing I was always moving closer to my goal, even if it wasn't from the direction I would've chosen. Sometimes we have a choice, and sometimes we don't.

If I wanted to be a mum, given our current fertility challenges, I needed to undergo fertility treatment, and I had no choice but to surrender to the experience. *Trust the process,* I told myself. Easy enough to say, but not so easy to do once the setbacks start to stack.

From this point, it was clear that both would-be parents need to be growing together. One parent can't just be all in with the work; both parents need to be all in.

I began to question whether I'd ever be a mum. Every time my period came, it felt like a death in the family. Hopes shattered. Another devastating failure. Was it even worth trying? For 3 years, we did the same dance, trusting the process, getting our hopes up, and being disappointed again and again. I was showing up, listening to the experts, and doing everything in my power to make each procedure a success, but it was never enough. When you're giving everything and it's not enough, it's downright demoralising.

It wasn't until Kevin and I decided it didn't matter how we became parents that I was truly able to let go and surrender to the experience. I became a student of the journey, realising that I was already embodying the mother archetype in other parts of my life. The birthing of my business was a creative act that took place in the womb space. Even if I couldn't have a child of my own in the way I wanted, I could still be a mum to our two dogs, a caring friend, a loving wife, and a compassionate sister. I didn't need a child to express those motherly traits. I was already a mum in my own way.

Finally, I accepted that I couldn't run from the problem. I couldn't change reality. Instead, I learnt to lean into the pain, accepting it as part of my journey and knowing I'd be stronger in the end.

> Don't run from your problems. You'll only end up running into them later down the track in a much more catastrophic way. You're much better off facing them head-on with a warrior's heart.

THE ART OF SLOWING DOWN… FROM TIME TO TIME

After facing my demons and continuing to fight for what I wanted in life, finally I was about to become a mum – a dream come true! I had put everything into The Search Republic and my personal brand, and suddenly my attention was about to be divided. I didn't want to be forced to neglect my business and end up resenting motherhood. I was facing a huge transitional period in my life, and I needed to ensure I found balance after the birth. So much was about to be out of my control, and I had to let go and allow it all to happen. *Okay, you know what you need to do. Trust the process. You've got this.* Our fertility journey taught me to surrender, and it was an approach I'd also need for the birth. *If I refuse to surrender to the experience, I'm going to get the biggest slap in the face…*

I decided I would give myself 40 days after the birth before I did anything work-related. I didn't need to be on my emails or any of the other platforms we use to communicate within the business. I knew the business wouldn't burn down while I was gone. At least, I had to trust that it wouldn't.

For me, slowing down wouldn't be easy. I had spent years in the rhythm of running my business, being in control, and constantly working, working, working. Suddenly, I was moving from a high-performance activity – running a business – to being a mum to a newborn baby. The time had come for a tempo change, but I wasn't sure if I was ready to slow down. It wasn't that I couldn't step away from the business and have it run smoothly without me; it was that I didn't want to. I love what I do, and stepping back would mean temporarily removing something I enjoy from my life. When I'm not working, like on weekends, I set a strong boundary for myself and my family. My weekends are sacred time for recharging, and I enjoy the downtime. No matter how much I love the work, it's not healthy to be in the business 24/7. By Monday, I'm raring to go, so the break ultimately does me good. But… how was I going to handle maternity leave? It would be a much bigger break than I was used to. *It's only 40 days,* I told myself, *and it's something I need to do. Surrender to the experience, and the business will still be there when I'm ready to return.*

Realising I still love what I do was reassuring before having a baby. Once my 40 days of maternity leave was over, I knew I'd be itching to dive back into the business headfirst. In a healthy, balanced way, of course.

EMBRACE PAST ADVERSITIES

When I look back at the past, I don't do so with regret or remorse, even when I'm thinking about my most difficult and traumatic moments. In fact, I appreciate those moments more than any other. They generated the pressure required to force me to become something stronger and more resilient than I was before. They forged my warrior spirit.

So many of us have overcome so much in our lives. Some of it almost broke us. All of it helped forge the stronger, wiser, more resilient people we are today. Can you think of a difficult situation you thought you couldn't get through but ultimately did? You might have several. At the time, it might have seemed like the end of the world. It might have felt like something you'd never recover from. The ultimate purpose of your greatest challenges might not have been clear at the time. However, looking back, can you now see why you had to experience them?

> Often, it's difficult to see the positives in negative moments as they're happening. Only by looking back do we understand the growth that was taking place.

God, imagine if I was still in a relationship with that person. Imagine if I was still friends with that person. Imagine if I didn't leave that job… We all have a string of difficult moments in our pasts that took us to where we are today. Broken relationships, lost jobs, health issues, financial issues, the deaths of loved ones – they all form part of the people we are today, hopefully for the better. The positives are there, but you must be prepared to see, acknowledge, and accept them.

INNER WARFARE: AN ACTIVITY TO AWAKEN YOUR WARRIOR

Relinquish Control

If you're a control freak like me, accepting that sometimes you need to surrender and let the cards fall how they will isn't easy. At the start of our fertility journey, I thought I could control the outcome if I just did the right research, bought the right supplements, and made all the right moves. As it turned out, it was a lot more complicated than that, and I was forced to hand much of the control over to others and the will of the universe.

Of course, I still did everything in my power to facilitate the process. Showing up is important. You can't just sit back and expect the universe to magically provide everything you need.

However, you must be ready to surrender to the process when the outcome is out of your control.

Are there any areas in your life where you're trying to exert control even though the outcome is out of your hands? I want you to think long and hard, and **write down** your responses. These are the areas in your life where you need to learn to surrender to the experience the most. If you've already done everything in your power to tilt the odds in your favour, fighting against the will of the universe at this point will only tire you out. You're best saving that energy for where it can actually make an impact.

Areas Where I Need to Surrender

....

....

....

....

....

....

....

....

....

I'm not going to ask you to do anything complicated here. If you've identified areas in your life where you need to surrender, I want you to reflect on your answers and imagine yourself lying back, letting go, and drifting with the current of the universe, going wherever it may take you. Remember, whatever happens was meant to be, and the outcome you want may not be the outcome you need. Just know, as Gabby Bernstein says, the universe always has your back.

THE UNIVERSE IS GIVING YOU EXACTLY WHAT YOU NEED... FOR REAL

If I had fallen pregnant right after Kevin and I got married, my business wouldn't have been in good enough shape for me to comfortably step away. It wouldn't have been the beast it became, with a competent team to keep it alive and thriving while I was on maternity leave. Basically, the timing wouldn't have been great.

Based on my own experiences running a business while juggling parenthood, I've made it my mission to empower business owners to work smarter, not harder, so they can truly enjoy the moments that matter most with the people they love, without the constant stress of where the next lead or sale will come from.

Growing up, I witnessed my mum single-handedly raise three

children. There were struggles, but there were also moments of magic that taught me the true meaning of resilience and love. Watching her journey ignited a deep drive in me – not just to succeed, but to follow in mum's footsteps and create a life where my own children would never have to go without.

It took 3 years to fall pregnant with Saige. The challenges we faced became the very fuel for my growth, and my business gave me purpose when I needed it most. I've always known I was meant to be a mother, and now I see how the universe was guiding me all along. Sometimes life gives you exactly what you asked for, just not in the way you imagined.

When I started my business, I dreamed of being able to work around my kids – and now I'm living that dream. It's an incredible feeling to see my 'why' come full circle, knowing that every step of the journey had a purpose, especially the most challenging moments.

When I failed to fall pregnant again and again and again, I asked, *Why me? Why us? Why does it have to be so hard?* Looking back, I realise it absolutely was for the best. I know what it's like to have a parent who works a lot. To support us after Dad left, Mum worked so much. She did what she had to do to keep a roof over our heads. If I could help it, I didn't want to end up in a similar situation, slaving away in my business when I'd rather be spending time with my kids. Thankfully, our fertility journey ended up being a drawn-out process, and I fell pregnant at exactly the right time.

When my dad left us, I was devastated. For years, I struggled to understand or forgive him. Looking back, I realise it was exactly what needed to happen to give me the drive to succeed in life. Would my life have been better or worse if he had stayed? There's no way to know for sure, but right now I'm living a greater, more fulfilling life than I ever could have imagined. In the end, the universe gives us everything we need, especially the things we don't know we need.

Even when we think the universe is against us, it isn't. It's always working for us, but we don't often realise it until much later. If I had fallen pregnant earlier, I wouldn't have been able to create the balance I wanted in my life to best support our kids. I wanted to be present in their lives. The whole experience almost broke us, testing our relationship to its limits, but we kept showing up, even when we felt like giving up. We kept doing the dance of life, doing the work, growing stronger and more resilient with each setback, and eventually we got not only exactly what we wanted but also what we needed *when* we needed it. Everything occurred at the exact right time. The universe was the ultimate choreographer, ensuring that everything happened as it should.

When our first baby, Saige, finally arrived, we knew we'd be ready for the next set of challenges that came our way. We had already walked through the fire, and, when we considered everything we had been through, the prospect of parenthood wasn't daunting at all. We were more than ready.

SAIGE FAITH RAYMOND

At 1 am on 21 July 2022, I woke up with a very intense period-like pain, and I woke Kevin up to tell him I was in labour. "Should I get up?" he asked.

"No," I said. "Stay in bed. The baby will be here soon, and you'll need your energy."

I was adamant that the birth was to be as close to nature as possible, given that she was conceived by science. From 37 weeks, the medical experts were on my case reminding me I was carrying precious cargo, and they wanted to try and get her out as early as possible. I simply wasn't in a position to allow that to happen. I wanted Saige to come when she was ready. I attended the hospital every few days for continuous monitoring to ensure the baby was happy and healthy, which she was. My intuition from 36 weeks told me she was coming early. Reality is, I got mixed up with my impatience at waiting to meet her, as I had already waited 3 years. Once I hit 40 weeks, every day overdue felt like a month.

Because I was so vocal about our fertility journey, so many people were excited about Saige arriving, and the pressure I felt was immense. I received so many messages every day via text and on all social media platforms from caring people looking for baby news. I got to a point at 9 days overdue where I decided to completely step away from social media, lock myself away from the world, and give myself the space to go into spontaneous labour on my own. When it finally started to happen, I was relieved and excited. Here was *the* moment we'd been dreaming of.

I laboured at home for a total of 20 hours with my TENS machine and bounce ball, going back and forth in and out of the bath. Then I went to hospital. I was 8 cm dilated, so I assumed bubs wouldn't be far off. As it turned out, she wasn't quite ready yet, and I spent another 10 hours labouring without pain relief. My ultimate goal was to have a water birth, and I was in and out of the birth pool during labour. We had studied hypno birthing, and Kevin was an excellent support partner who kept saying the supportive affirmations to encourage me to get through it.

Then at 30 hours, I finally consented to an epidural and to having my waters broken to bring on labour. The epidural really helped, giving me a break from the pain. I badly needed to sleep, as, by this point, I had been awake for nearly 2 days with only 3 hours of sleep before going into labour. Both Hubby and I had an hour of sleep (Hubby slept on a mattress on the floor) and woke up feeling refreshed. I thought I would be pushing by then, but no, Saige was facing the wrong direction. She was facing my inner groin, and every time I had a contraction, she wasn't moving. The midwives thought she would drop into position, but she didn't. Six hours later, her heart rate dropped. Because she was in the wrong position, there was so much swelling in my uterus, which was causing complications. A few hours later, the midwives told me that if I tried to birth naturally, they could lose one of us, as the swelling could lead to me having a huge haemorrhage. Baby was stuck, and, at that point, an emergency C-section was the safest way to deliver her.

The estimated wait time was 3 hours, as there were others ahead of me on the surgery list, which would mean 23 July would be Saige's birthday, making her a Leo (she was right on the cusp of Cancer and Leo). Then 20 minutes later, the obstetricians came into the room in panic, saying, "We need to get this baby out now. Her heart rate is dropping."

At that stage, I was very eager and thankful to have a C-section, as I knew I had done everything in my power to get Saige out safely. Although the birth I wanted wasn't to be, at the end of the day, all I wanted was a happy, safe, healthy baby in my arms.

I was raced into theatre and within 10 minutes, our baby girl was born. The joy and love were insane. I had zero birth trauma, as I felt very in control of my choice. We were so in love with our new precious miracle. Our life was complete. We finally had everything we had wanted for so long right there in our arms. Everything was right in the world.

On Friday 22 July 2022 at 11:06 pm, after 46 hours of labour, our precious daughter, **Saige Faith Raymond,** arrived. She was almost 2 weeks overdue.

In the days that followed, my surgical scar kept weeping, so a week after Saige was born, I was readmitted. I had a 14 cm haematoma, and they needed to open me up and drain it so I could heal properly. I was glad to go back into hospital to get a break from all the visitors and also to rest and soak up the newborn bubble.

From the day Saige was born, she was an incredible sleeper. She slept 4–5 hours at a time, making the transition to parenthood so smooth and enjoyable while allowing me time to recover.

When I was 14 weeks pregnant, we chose the name Saige, which represents healing and wisdom. It was a long labour – 46 hours is no joke! – but I'd do it all again in a heartbeat to have her with us.

From the start, she was a chilled baby who loved her food and cuddles, and was in no rush to do anything, which explains why she kept us waiting to meet her for 41 weeks and 4 days. She took so long to arrive Earthside that she missed the newborn stage and went right into 000 (0–3 months) clothes.

Nothing could have prepared me for the immense love I felt for my baby girl. Often, waves of pure love wash over me, filling me with pure joy because she is here with us Earthside. I feel incredibly honoured and privileged that she chose us as her parents. Saige has filled our hearts with an abundance of love, bliss, purpose, and sheer happiness. Becoming her mumma has fulfilled my life's purpose. After all the frustration, perseverance, and growth, we finally had our beautiful baby girl. It was a dream come true.

Since becoming a mother, I have discovered that the person I am now is who I was always meant to be. Saige and Willow (our second daughter) were the missing pieces that completed our happily ever after story.

During our fertility fight, I learnt that no matter how much I want something, no matter how self-motivated I am, there's a natural timing and process to everything. After everything we had been through, after a long journey, having a family was the best gift we could have asked for. But they didn't arrive on my timeline; they came when they were ready. In the end, they came when *we* were ready.

In life and business, things won't always happen how and when you want them too. While you do need to put in the work and sometimes fight for what you want, don't assume it automatically means you'll get it. It's not how it works. There are always outside forces at play, and understanding this, accepting it, and surrendering is key. Trust that the universe always has your back.

THE FIRST 40 DAYS

My post-birth recovery was more complicated than I imagined. Honestly, I had a difficult labour – a full 46 hours, remember? – which was taxing on my body, so recovery was slow. Even so, labour wasn't the toughest experience of my life. Thankfully, all my past struggles had built a level of strength and resilience in me that absolutely helped when it came time to bring my baby Earthside.

The problem was, I wasn't used to sitting still, and I wasn't taking my recovery as seriously as I should have. In typical Sonja fashion, I overdid it with visitors and outings with our new pride and joy, and after ending up back in hospital a week after having Saige and requiring surgery, I decided to slow down completely and enjoy my time with Saige. Fortunately, she was happy, healthy, and super chilled, so my introduction to motherhood was a pleasant experience.

If I wanted to bounce back quicker, I needed to focus on my recovery instead of trying to do too much too soon, which meant minimal visitors and social outings. I found it difficult to do in practice. But after the intense labour, I was running on empty, and I needed to refill my tank so I could be the best mum, wife, and business owner I could be. I had to find the balance between being the go-getter and the present mother, embracing the stillness of being a new mum.

From my research, I knew that the first 40 days postpartum were crucial for healing, re-energising, and switching back to pre-pregnancy mode. At the same time, this period helps your baby adjust to living outside your womb and bond with you face to face. The first 40 days of life can impact the next 40 years. The more healing intention I could bring to our lives now, the better our physical, mental, and emotional health would be later.

I had worked so hard to bring Saige into the world, from the beginning of our fertility journey to her birth, and I didn't want to leave anything to chance, which was why I hired not one but two postpartum doulas to support me with my transition during the first 40 days of motherhood, known as matrescence. When a baby is born, a mother is also born.

THE SEARCH FOR MY MARY POPPINS

As I eased back into work, I realised I'd need some extra help with Saige if I wanted to give 100 percent to my business. Essentially, I needed a Mary Poppins, someone who would become an extension of our family. And so, the search began.

After conducting ten interviews over a week, I found the perfect person for the role. I found our Mary Poppins, and she was 'practically perfect' in every single way. In the process, I also found two backup babysitters, so creating my support village was something I could tick off my list.

I can't stress how important it is to have the right support around you in both business and life. Being from Ireland, I didn't have much family in Australia, aside from my sister who didn't live close by. I also have some amazing friends who are practically like family. I wasn't totally alone, but I did need the extra support my Mary Poppins provided.

There are no gold medals for trying to go it alone. We all need support from time to time. My postpartum experience was very peaceful, and I put it down to Saige being super chilled in nature and having the right support around me in my two doulas as well. It made me realise how important additional support would be moving forward. Why do it the hard way if I didn't have to?

When I was working, I was able to give everything to my business and my clients because I knew I had the best person possible looking after our daughter. When I was with Saige, I was able to be completely present because I had handled all the work stuff within work hours. Being a new mumma, I had less time than ever to complete tasks and work towards goals, which meant I had to be super strict about where I spent my time, and anything that relieved some of the pressure was more than welcome.

I didn't have to go back into my business as soon as I did, but I chose to return earlier than perhaps some new mothers do because, let's face it, I'm not the person to sit around looking at four walls, especially when Saige slept for 4.5 hours at a time. I also had goals I wanted to achieve before the end of the year. I'm so grateful that our Mary Poppins and others in our little support village give me the freedom to keep kicking professional goals. I worked at home and breastfed my baby for 13 months, so having a nanny allowed me to work around her nursing needs and be present in between meetings.

Honestly, one of my limiting beliefs was that I didn't think I could run a successful business as a new mum. Early in the pregnancy, I often thought about the kind of mum I wanted to be and who I would become. My goal was to never give up on my dreams and never lose sight of who I was deep down. Once I became a mum, I chose to embrace my new identity as a mumpreneur.

During my first month back in the business, we had a record month in terms of revenue and profit. Not what I expected, but a welcomed surprise and confirmation that I was doing something right. As it turned out, with the right support, I could be both a present mother and a successful business owner.

Since becoming a mum, I'm more conscious about looking after myself first so I have more to give. I've now proven that we can have it all in life. It all comes down to asking quality questions to get quality answers. *How will I make it happen?* As Tony Robbins said, "The quality of your life is a direct reflection of the quality of the questions you are asking yourself." Ask the right questions, and you'll get the right answers.

I made mumpreneurship work, and I feel blessed for the situation I'm in. Don't get me wrong, I do have tough days. Being a mumpreneur isn't all smooth sailing, but I've built enough resilience over the years to get me through the difficult times, knowing that smoother seas are always on the horizon. On the toughest days, I find it useful to focus on my *why* and *big vision* for my life. I also practise gratitude to help balance my emotions. The right support is crucial, whether that be people or go-to tools to help manage my mindset.

FIVE TIPS FOR NAVIGATING PARENT LIFE AS A MUMPRENEUR (OR OTHER WORKING PROFESSIONAL)

After all the years I've spent as a professional in my industry, running my own business, and all the personal development work I've done, the thing that really drove home the concept of using my time more efficiently was becoming a mum. Parenthood changes everything.

Through trial and error, I came up with a list of actions that helped me (and can help you if you find yourself in a similar situation) reclaim some of your time and ensure you're looking out for number one – because being a great parent and a successful professional is difficult when you're not meeting your own needs.

So, here are my hottest tips, my most effective dance moves for navigating life as a mumpreneur, dadpreneur, or any other working professional:

1. **Make self-care a priority.** When you're responsible for others – baby, business, employees, and so on – to fully show up, you need to be healthy and well-rested. Easy to say, not always easy to achieve, I know. What are the non-negotiables in your self-care routine? How can you ensure you always fit them into your schedule? When you look after yourself, looking after others is a lot easier.

2. **If you don't have time to read, listen.** As a lover of mindset, biz growth, and personal development books, I fit them into my schedule by listening to the audiobook versions. Often, listening to a book is much more convenient than reading from a page. For example, I can consume an audiobook while driving, walking the dogs, or hitting the gym. Sure, it's not exactly the same as *reading* the text, but at least I can still get my book fix in audio form. It's small hacks like this that help reduce the number of sacrifices you need to make when giving your family and business the attention they deserve.

3. **Get out in nature.** As a species, we're meant to be in nature, and getting out in the fresh air, among the trees,

rivers, beaches, wherever you feel most content, is a crucial part of self-care. One study showed that spending at least 2 hours per week in nature has a positive impact on overall health and wellbeing.[13] Personally, my dogs give me a great excuse to regularly walk in nature, not that we should ever need an excuse to spend time in our natural environment.

4. **Share the load.** Like many entrepreneurs, I do have a tendency to take on everything myself – or at least try to – and refuse to ask for help. For example, I was inadvertently doing a disservice to both Hubby and our girls by taking on all the home and child duties myself. Eventually, I realised my error. Now, Daddy and the girls get their time together in the evenings, and I get to refill my cup – a win all round. Resist the urge to do it all yourself. When we do take on too much, it's rarely only us who suffers. Others are affected too.

5. **Find others in the same boat.** Even months after their births, I was still learning the girls' cues. As children do, they were constantly developing, and every day was a learning experience. Keeping up with all the seemingly sudden changes was difficult at times. But guess what? Other mums were in the exact same situation, which was why it was important to cultivate a village of support so we all had someone to lean on when times got tough. As parents, we're all doing the best we can with what we know, and sometimes we need others to remind us of that.

My five tips for busy mumpreneurs have worked for me, and I'm sure they'll work for others too, but that doesn't mean it needs to end there. Anything you can do to practise self-care and ensure you're fuelled and ready to handle all business and life have to throw at you should become a regular part of your routine. As they say, happy mum, happy bub, and happy business too.

THE HEART NEVER LIES

Throughout our fertility journey, we could have given up at any point – but we didn't. Why? Because we chose the battle that mattered. I knew that deep down being a mum was what my inner self truly wanted. Not everything you want will be worth a long and gruelling fight to achieve it. Sometimes giving up and moving on is the right decision.

When you're facing a tough battle for something you want, ask yourself, *Is it truly what my inner self wants? Will it really make me happy? Is it worth the fight?* You may not be able to answer these answers straight away. You may need to examine them closely, meditate on them, and try to understand what your inner self really wants. Asking deep questions in the morning – before you've touched your phone, spoken to anyone, or had any other outside influences – can help you get the right answers.

When all else fails, listen to your gut. It will tell you when you're on track and when you need to correct course. If something is draining you and the effort doesn't seem worth the reward, it might be time to step back or move on. On the other hand, if something is energising you and bringing you joy, you should lean into it. We know intuitively what's good for us and what's not. Your inner self has all the answers, but you must be willing to listen.

FACE EACH CHALLENGE WITH A WARRIOR'S HEART

Every obstacle we face in life is put in our path for a reason. Don't try to avoid them. To get the lesson, you must face and overcome each challenge. I've seen so many people, myself included, try to avoid rough waters only to end up on the rocks anyway.

> Showing up and surrendering doesn't mean not taking action. It doesn't mean not making decisions. Quite the opposite. It's about doing everything in your power and letting the universe take care of the rest.

Our fertility journey was the most difficult experience of my life. It's why I speak so openly about it. I know that other women are experiencing similar battles, and I wanted to shed light on what some consider a taboo subject. I want them to know they're not alone. While we may feel like we need to go it alone, we're doing a disservice to ourselves when we don't seek support. My greatest achievements are my two girls, Saige and Willow (more about Willow soon). I feel blessed to have gone through and overcome such a challenging experience.

Looking back, even though we had a difficult 3-year journey, I genuinely wouldn't change it for the world. I'm not just saying it now because I've made it through to the other side stronger, happier, more resilient than ever. It's true that when we overcome our biggest challenges, the ones we swear would break us, we often look back and realise, as cliché as it sounds, everything happens for a reason. All the synchronicities make perfect sense, and it couldn't have happened any other way. I asked for a business, I got one. I asked for a baby, and I was blessed with two miracle babies. I asked for a lifestyle to work around my kids; yep, I got it. In the end, I got everything I asked for, just not in the way I expected.

Of course, the universe didn't simply hand me everything I wanted. I had to work to receive it, showing up for myself again and again, pushing myself beyond what I thought I could handle. During our fertility journey, my business was my biggest blessing. While at a certain point I couldn't control the outcome of my quest to become a mum, I could throw myself wholeheartedly into my business and build something great. Call it a distraction, call it unconventional therapy, call it whatever you want – but when Saige and Willow finally arrived, I was grateful to have built something that could support us as a family and allow me the time and space to connect with my daughters.

Before starting my business, I wouldn't have had the confidence to speak about our fertility journey. I wouldn't have had the confidence to put myself out there online and onstage. I wouldn't have had the confidence to write this book. Everything that has happened in my life – the good, the bad, and the ugly – has pushed me closer to where I needed to be, even if I didn't realise it until later.

Through sharing my journey on social media, I built strong connections with people who became dear friends and dear clients. My words resonated with them, and if I didn't keep showing up, even on the days when I didn't want to, none of this would have happened. I wouldn't be living my ideal life with so many amazing people in it.

If you touch just one person with your story, you've made an impact. You may have made someone's day. You may have changed their life. When I started talking about my deepest fears and darkest shadows, I received message after message of thanks. *I really needed to hear that today,* many of them said.

> **Not everything is sunshine and rainbows, and you can't avoid the harsh reality of life forever. Eventually, you will need to face your demons and, with strength, courage, and resilience, defeat them. To win, you must be willing to fight.**

Often, the people who have an avoidant nature and try to skirt around their problems aren't great at making their own decisions. They're constantly focused on the opinions of others and struggle to think for themselves.

> If you're avoiding obstacles and letting others direct you, not only are you not getting what you want in life, but you're also not evolving. You're not testing yourself. You're not building resilience. You're living as a follower, not a warrior.

Each challenge is a blessing in disguise, so embrace each obstacle in your path and recognise them for what they are – opportunities for growth. Trust the journey and don't get upset when your plans fall apart. Often, the universe has a much bigger and better plan for us than what we imagined for ourselves. The key is to surrender and accept it.

We spend so much time distracted by our phones, social media, everything going on in our lives that we forget about the underlying magic of the universe. Trees growing, babies being born, gravity, the body's natural healing ability – it's all as awe-inspiring as actual magic, but we often don't notice, and we take it for granted.

> A power exists far beyond our understanding, and we must embrace it and trust in the process if we want to be content in life.

I do feel the energy of the universe, and I feel that we're all connected. Just because we can't see that connection, it doesn't mean it's not there. You simply have to show up, surrender, and trust that everything that happens in your life, even your most traumatic experiences, serve a greater purpose. They're shaping you into the strong resilient warrior you're destined to become.

Show Up and Surrender to the Experience

1. Do everything in your power, then surrender. Once you've done everything in your power to achieve a certain outcome, there's nothing more to do other than surrender to the experience and let the universe provide what it will. You may not get what you want, but you'll always get what you need.

2. Every obstacle is a necessary part of your journey. Each challenge you face, especially the most difficult and seemingly insurmountable, help forge the warrior you must become. Through struggle, we build strength. In fact, it's the only way.

3. The universe works on its own timeline. Your proposed timeline might not match that of the universe. What you believe is the right timing may not actually be ideal, although seeing this can be difficult. When in doubt, trust that the universe always has your back.

4. We all need support. In business and in life, we all need support from time to time. Don't be afraid to ask for help when you need it. As much as you might be driven to do everything yourself, you simply can't.

5. Take care of yourself to better support others. Want to show up for your friends, family, and business in the best way possible? It all starts with self-care. To effectively support others, you must support yourself first. Self-care is critical.

Don't be afraid
to unleash your
authentic self
on the world.

AWAKENING THE WARRIOR

9

VANQUISH SENSELESS FEAR AND ANXIETY

RULE-BREAKERS AND RISK-TAKERS

When I first started my business, I was afraid to put myself out there. For the entire first year, I flew under the radar. I didn't have a website, and few people knew I was even trading. Sure, word got around, but I didn't publicly announce anything for a long time. Why? Because I was so afraid of being judged. *Who do I think I am, going out on my own? What makes me think I can run a business? Why would anyone want to work with me?* Even though I had all the right qualifications and experience, the fear, anxiety, and negative self-talk were real.

Tall poppy syndrome is a big issue in my home country of Ireland. When people see others excelling, they try to cut them down. No one is supposed to grow too tall. While people are often encouraged to go to uni, which is the main avenue to get a good job, they aren't really encouraged to make something of themselves. They aren't encouraged to rise above the other poppies in the field. Anyone who dares to dream too big and grow too tall is swiftly cut down to size. "Who does she think she is?" they say. Consequently, I didn't just have a fear of failure but also a fear of success. I was afraid to stand out and stand too tall because I didn't want to get cut down. Thriving in an environment where success is seen as a fault isn't easy, which is why my move to Australia was such a critical point in my life. Naturally, a lot of fear and anxiety comes up when you leave your home country to live on the other side of the world, but for me the risk seemed well worth the potential reward, and I haven't looked back.

In Australia, I've met the most amazing businesswomen and friends that I call my chosen family. I wouldn't have got to where I am today without all the love and encouragement I've received from those in my network. It gives me the drive to keep pushing towards even bigger goals because I know that the people around me are there to support me, not compete with me or try to take me down. In Australia, I've witnessed more of an abundance mindset rather than the austerity mindset I experienced in Ireland. I feel encouraged to stand out, grow tall, and keep reaching for my goals. No one is demanding that I conform to strict societal standards. Instead, they're cheering me on, elevating me to new and exciting heights.

Throughout our lives, especially in mainstream schooling, we're conditioned to stand in line, fit in, and remain uniform. Face the front. Listen to the teacher. Don't you dare speak out of turn. The same rules often flow into the workplace. Standing out and speaking up can be career suicide, as I eventually learnt. In school, I didn't follow the rules, and I was frequently kicked out of class. If I stood up, I was told to sit back down. If I spoke up, I was told to shut up. There was no room in the classroom for unconventional opinions. People who challenged the status quo were too disruptive, and their opinions needed to be shut down immediately when really they should have been explored and even nurtured.

I don't see following rules that you don't agree with as a positive. In fact, it can lead to the unravelling of your inner self. It can stop you from doing what you're meant to do and being who you're meant to be. What keeps us following all the nonsensical rules people force upon us? Fear mongering. The rule-makers want everyone marching to the same beat. They want to control us. They don't want us taking any risks.

> But being a rule-breaker and risk-taker is the ultimate freedom. Suddenly, you're in control of your own life, which is the way it should be.

When you try something new, you'll likely experience some fear and anxiety. It's normal, natural, but it doesn't need to stop you from getting what you want in life. Even after I overcame the initial fear of starting The Search Republic, I still felt anxiety around every new undertaking within the business. For example, in 2021, when I began setting up my first ever online program for people who don't have the budget for my done-for-you services, I hit a wall of limiting beliefs I thought I had already overcome. *What if I don't know what I'm doing? What if no one is interested in the program? What if it isn't a success?* Sound familiar? This also happened in 2024 when I set up my group program The Growth Movement. The fear and anxiety weren't rational. Of course, I knew how to make a valuable program, and of course I knew people would be scrambling to sign up if I got the messaging right. I wasn't making the program on a whim. I knew my market, and I knew that the program was something people wanted.

In a way, you need to be your own internal coach, working through fear and anxiety when they arise – because they're almost never justified. **When I did start putting myself and my business out there, all the negative self-talk melted away because I felt validated by my success. I had proven the voice in my head wrong. My only regret was that I let fear hold me back for so long. I should have started my business sooner.**

Are fear and anxiety stopping you from doing something powerful and important? Don't let them. The time to work through it is now. The sooner you do, the sooner you can start moving towards your goal.

MY MOST TERRIFYING MOMENT IN BUSINESS

On 3 March 2021, I was preparing to do my first ever Facebook Live. Since starting my business 3 years prior, I had been avoiding doing Lives and any face-to-face camera stories. Why? As I'm sure you can guess, fear and anxiety were holding me back. Finally, however, it was time to face those fears, and the camera, head-on.

In the lead-up to going live, my heart was pounding so hard in my chest that I could feel my pulse in my ears like bongo drums… *da dum, da dum, da dum.* My ears started ringing with a deafening high-pitched sound. My hands were clammy with sweat. I felt so dizzy. *Am I about to vomit?* The heat rose from my toes to my throat – I felt like a saucepan that was about to boil over. I felt like I was going to pass out. Then the negative self-talk started. *Who do you think you are, Sonja? Who wants to listen to what you have to say? What makes you think you've got anything worth saying?* The nasty voice in my head was relentless.

I started bawling uncontrollably. I wanted to run, run away from the vengeful spirit that was haunting my thoughts. It was a spirit that had followed me since childhood, a time when I constantly lived in fear. One particular traumatic memory comes to mind when examining where my current fears and anxieties came from. One day at school, when I was 14 years old, I planned to go out for lunch with one of my friends. However, a girl in my class informed me that a gang of girls were waiting at the school gate to beat me up. Why? I didn't know. No one knew. I didn't even know who they were. To avoid putting myself in danger, I told my friend I didn't feel well and stayed at school for lunch. I was terrified, almost frozen in fear. *Why is this happening to me?* That fear stuck with me for a long time.

When it came time to do my Facebook Live, I felt that old fear resurface. It was a fear of being judged and the consequences that would follow. It came back to haunt me because I had never fully dealt with it. Clearly, there was a lesson I was yet to learn. In that moment, I realised I had some serious work to do on myself, which I did eventually do. However, I also had a Live to do, so I had to find a way to push through the fear then and there. I told myself that what I was feeling now wasn't the same as what I felt back then. There was no one waiting nearby to physically hurt me. I was simply being triggered by my past, and it was time to move on. But could I do it?

The Facebook Live was titled 'Fear of Judgement'. Fitting,

right? I managed to push through, discussing how it was my first ever Live and being open about my fear of being judged. My subconscious told me it was dangerous, and it was by far the scariest thing I had done in my business. I could've easily backed out. I could've chosen to believe the BS story I was telling myself. Instead, I acknowledged the fear, pushed through it, and successfully completed my first Facebook Live, which went amazingly. Afterwards, I felt a strong sense of empowerment. For years, I had let that old fear control me. I never felt like I was good enough. What a load of BS! Did I receive a beating afterwards? Nope. What I did receive were the most beautiful words of encouragement from people watching, thanking me for sharing my message. Finally, my true inner voice spoke, overriding the vengeful spirit of fear that had taunted me for so long. *I knew you could do it. What were you afraid of? You're amazing!*

Now I want to turn it back to you. Have you had any similar experiences where your fears paralysed you, preventing you from taking the necessary steps in your personal or professional life? Did you suppress those fears to avoid discomfort? Or did you face them to reach your goal? Were any of those fears, like mine, the result of past trauma?

We have a tendency to bury our trauma and not deal with it head-on because it's too painful to face. The reality is, until we address the root cause, the trauma will show up in other ways, ultimately causing more damage. As hard as it may seem, we must make peace with our trauma to move beyond it.

On my entrepreneurial journey, fear paralysed me many

times. However, the day of my first Facebook Live was when I chose to kick fear to the curb. Exactly 2 years later, I conquered another fear, standing on stage as a keynote speaker at International Women's Day in 2023 in Crown Towers in Perth to share our fertility journey. It was a very vulnerable moment, but I didn't let the fear and anxiety stop me from taking the stage. I'd never let fear rule my life again. I've now spoken at countless events, and 'keynote speaker' has become a big part of my identity, with public speaking now a familiar and fulfilling dance, but it wouldn't have come to be if I hadn't taken the leap and conquered that initial fear. The way I see it, my message isn't about me. It's about how I can help people, and it needs to be shared.

> A successful brand doesn't come to be without doing the inner work, and my business has been the vehicle for me to deal with my inner demons. Overcoming my fear of judgement and putting myself out there ramped up not only my self-confidence but my business as well.

Why did I wait so long to put myself in front of the camera? From the moment I got over myself, got out of my own way, and made my business about the people I could help, everything changed for the better.

The demons that emerged during that first Facebook Live horrified me, and it was a clear sign that I needed to invest in myself and start doing the inner work. The event was a major catalyst for a lot of the self-development work I ended up doing.

With fear kicked aside, I was free to focus on my vision and what I was here to do. I was no longer hiding from my demons but facing them head-on when they appeared. Since that first Facebook Live, my mantra has been, "It's my job to be the light, despite the chaos. I must guide the way."

> The only way to defeat the darkness is to shine a light on it. We can't conquer our fears until we're willing to face them.

EVERY JOURNEY BEGINS WITH A FIRST STEP

What would you do right now if you knew in advance you couldn't fail? Why aren't you doing it? Sure, failure is a possibility, but so is success. How can you achieve success if you aren't willing to fail?

Too many people don't even take the first step towards their biggest dreams for fear of failure. I've been guilty of this multiple times, from starting my business to going live on Facebook for the first time. While the fear of failure may never fully go away, I've learnt that it's a baseless fear. If you fail, so what? What's the worst that could happen? Do you fear that others will judge you for failing? Vanquish that fear right now. In fact, if the people around you aren't ready to cheer you on, whether you're succeeding or not, it's time to reassess who you're spending your time with. Neglecting your dreams for fear of judgement is betraying your true self to appeal to others. Don't shrink yourself down and let the crowd swallow you. You're meant to be different, and you don't need to blend in. Who you are is a gift, so don't squander it. Instead, take action to chase your dreams and stay true to yourself.

Often, the biggest hurdle in any scary endeavour is the first step. Once you start down a certain path, you realise it's not so scary after all and you're much more capable than you thought. Trust me. Been there. Learnt that lesson. Even so, it's a lesson I need to remind myself of whenever I step out of my comfort zone and attempt something new. When fear of failure freezes you in place, keeping you from your goals, the key is to notice what's happening and call it out for what it is – your ego trying to protect you. Your ego is like an overprotective mother. It wants to protect you from adversity, not realising that adversity is a catalyst for growth.

To avoid an ego block, take consistent and immediate action towards your goal. Even small steps move you forward. As long as you're in constant motion, you will reach your destination eventually.

While it seems hard to believe now, I once had a fear of public speaking. As a now-accomplished keynote speaker, I've since taken the stage multiple times, and people pay to hear me speak and are interested in what I have to say. While there are sometimes nerves, I no longer feel full-blown fear. I've proven that I'm up to the task. Conquering my fear of public speaking meant having a stern word with my overprotective ego and taking the plunge. My first Facebook Live was a stepping stone to the stage, and it helped me push through my limiting beliefs.

The story I told myself played a big part in my fear. *I have a fear of public speaking.* Was it even a real fear? Or was I simply creating the fear from a baseless story, like a self-fulfilling prophecy? I don't even know where the limiting belief came from. But now that I've overcome it, just try and keep me off the stage. By changing the story in my head, I changed the story of my life, and you can do the same.

If I hadn't had the courage to face my fear of failure over and over again, I wouldn't have achieved my biggest dreams. I wouldn't have moved to Australia and crossed paths with my future husband. I wouldn't be running a successful business. I wouldn't have my beautiful daughters. As Wayne Gretzky said, "You miss 100 percent of the shots you don't take."

What have you been putting off for fear of failure? That fear ends today. You don't need to see the whole staircase to take the first step. You just need the courage to take it.

INNER WARFARE: AN ACTIVITY TO AWAKEN YOUR WARRIOR

Unmasking Fear and Anxiety

Whenever fear and anxiety try to take over my thoughts, I ask myself, *What's the worst that could happen?* If I'm hesitant to try something new and exciting, I ask, *What's the worst that could happen? Seriously, how bad could it be?* Once I have my answer, I decide whether I could handle the worst possible outcome or not. If not, I reconsider whether I'm making the right move. If I can handle the worst, then there's nothing stopping me from moving forward, so I take the step forward.

But we shouldn't just dwell on the negatives. I also like to imagine the best possible outcome. *What will it look like if I succeed? Are the risks worth the possible reward?* If the answer is yes, then I have even more of a reason to move forward.

Is fear and anxiety holding you back from taking action in your life, career, or business? I want you to consider all the important moves you've been hesitant to make. **Write them down**. Now I want you to imagine the worst-case scenario if you fail. Could you handle it? **Write down your answer.** Now I want you to imagine the best-case scenario if you succeed. Is the risk worth the reward? **Write down your answer.**

For example, when I was considering starting my own

business, fear of failure held me back. So, for **action**, I'd write: *Starting my business*. When I considered the worst-case scenario, being broke and having to go back to work for someone else – I realised I could handle it. If I didn't make the move, I'd be stuck working for someone else anyway, and being broke would only be temporary if my business failed. So, for **could you handle the worst-case scenario?** I'd write: *Yes*. Then I considered the best-case scenario… success! *Wow, how good does that look?* To me, the risk was well worth the reward, and thankfully I got to see my best-case scenario play out. In fact, it was even better than I imagined. So, for **is the risk worth the reward?** I'd write: *Yes*.

Now it's your turn to use your imagination to remove some fear, anxiety, and doubt from your life.

Action	Could you handle the worst-case scenario?	Is the risk worth the reward?

Action	Could you handle the worst-case scenario?	Is the risk worth the reward?

Were your fears justified? Or are you now inspired to take meaningful action to achieve your goals? Remember, your inner self has all the answers. The key is to listen, examine, and act. You've got this.

VULNERABILITY IS A BUILDING BLOCK OF RESILIENCE

During my business, fertility, and motherhood journeys, I've learnt that sometimes we have to admit something is hard before we can get through it. **Your warrior spirit may compel you to always put on a brave face and never admit that times are tough when adversity strikes, but sometimes doing so can be detrimental to your progress.**

We often think of vulnerability as weakness, and we fear being vulnerable around others. But in reality, vulnerability is a sign of strength. It takes courage to open up and show our true selves to others, especially when we're not sure how they'll respond. The truth? Laying it bare can be incredibly empowering.

While it took me some time to get to a point where I could be openly vulnerable – the stubborn Irish lass in me took some persuading – I no longer have a problem with vulnerability and have found it to be a critical part of building resilience.

> When we embrace vulnerability,
> we allow ourselves to connect with
> others on a deeper level.

We create space for empathy and understanding, and we show others that it's okay to be imperfect. I've been vulnerable online and onstage, baring my soul to the world, and it's no longer something I'm afraid to do, as I'm healed from the trauma. *What will people think if I admit how much I've struggled? How will they judge me?* Those thoughts and fears have been vanquished because I've witnessed the awesome power of vulnerability.

As someone who often stands before hundreds of awe-inspiring women, laying bare my struggles with fertility and starting my business, I know firsthand how freeing airing your vulnerability is. Is it risky? Maybe, but I've found that not only does sharing your vulnerability take a huge load off, but it's also a bridge to trust. Now just to be clear, I would only suggest that people be fully vulnerable once they have healed or have come full-circle and learnt the lesson so they don't go around 'trauma dumping' on others. It can be a fine line, and that's why doing the inner work is so important.

Opening up, sharing your vulnerability, and showing up as your authentic self not only benefits you but also your business in several ways:

- Humanises your business and strengthens your bonds with clients.
- Fosters authentic connections with prospective clients.

- Does wonders for your relatability and empathy.
- Transfers to your brand, increasing client trust in your business.
- Shows that you're not afraid of self-reflection and transparency.

Gabby Bernstein said it best: "When we feel safe enough to expose our shadows, that's when we become free." I couldn't agree more.

THE RIGHT TOOL FOR EVERY OCCASION

One of my biggest fears in life was not being able to be a mum. I quickly learnt that our fears can control us, and my fears around fertility were making it harder for me to fall pregnant. I wasn't facing my demons, and I wasn't surrendering to the grand plan of the universe. Instead, I was ignoring the root of my anxieties and fighting unwinnable battles.

My other biggest fear was a fear of dying. I know that's probably a common one, but it was a big deal for me. When you're afraid of death, it can distract you from living. While fear is useful when it helps you avoid or overcome potentially dangerous situations, unfounded fear can be a curse. I'm not saying dying isn't scary – I'm sure it is – but it's also inevitable. Why fear the inevitable? We all die. It's a fact of life. You can't stop it, so why fear it? When you fear the inevitable, you waste energy that would be better spent on things within your control.

Fear of death was a curse I carried for years, and psychedelics helped me overcome it. How? Well, when you take a big enough dose of certain substances – like 5-MeO DMT, also known as toad – you completely leave your body. It feels like you've died. Now that I know what it feels like to die, I'm not afraid of dying anymore. It's not as scary as I thought. I know psychedelics aren't for everyone, and there are other ways to work through your fears. Make sure you're asking the right questions. You know the process… What are you afraid of? What's the worst that could happen? Could you handle that? Is this right for you? When it comes to psychedelics, you really need to be prepared and ready for what you could experience. It's certainly not for everyone.

While psychedelics were a powerful tool for me, they alone weren't enough. I needed a complete repertoire of supportive elements that would help me deal with everyday fears and anxieties. It wasn't until I started reading self-help books and working with Tony Robbins that I began to feel like I was learning the right moves. They weren't moves they taught us in school. They weren't moves my parents showed me. To learn these powerful new dance moves, I had to seek them out from those who had mastered them before me.

While Tony Robbins worked for me, he's not the only person out there offering self-development. There are loads of people to choose from who can help you acquire what you need to move through your fears and anxieties.

Ultimately, you can't change the people around you. You can't change society. You can't change reality. You can, however, change yourself and ensure you've always got a repertoire of support to move through all of life's challenges.

Once I conquered my fear of not being a mum and fear of dying, I no longer felt stuck in place. My ego was no longer holding me back, trying to protect me. By facing my fears, they lost their power over me, melting away like an ice cube in a glass of water on a hot day, never to be solid again.

FERTILITY JOURNEY ROUND TWO

On 3 December 2023, I was scheduled for another embryo transfer. That's right – we were going for baby number two!

In the weeks leading up to the procedure, some old fears and anxieties rose to the surface. Apparently, they weren't as conquered as I had thought. The trauma from our very first scan all those years ago that identified the silent miscarriage stuck with me. I was worried the embryo transfer would fail and I'd be forced to relive that traumatic experience, learning we'd lost the baby, suddenly bleeding through my jeans in my office, and rushing home to clean myself up before an Instagram Live. Yeah, I wasn't eager to repeat that experience.

As Christmas drew closer, I began to feel calmer. I already had Saige, so another baby would simply be a blessing. Even so, I would've loved nothing more than for it to work. During our fertility journey, we had a few Christmases that were consumed with sadness as another year wound down with no baby in my tummy. I didn't want to have another one of those sad Christmases.

Instead, I wanted to be happy and content knowing I'd soon be a mum to another perfect baby.

I'll admit, not being able to fall pregnant in the conventional sense still got to me. *Why do some couples have it so easy? They just have sex, and suddenly they have a baby on the way.* To avoid overthinking, I kept myself busy and tried to take control of my anxiety, telling myself to once again surrender to the experience and trust the process. *What will be will be.*

I felt incredibly grateful to have Saige. My heart burst with the love I have for her, and I knew I had the capacity to love another child just as much. Why wouldn't a baby want to come and be with us? We had built a beautiful home and life for us and our kids. We had dealt with most of our demons. We were born to be great parents.

In the lead-up to the latest embryo transfer, I did a lot of work on myself. I did psychedelics again, energy work, and acupuncture. I dieted and lost some weight and took a holiday, getting myself in the best physical and mental state possible. I set up my business in a way that created space for another baby. Essentially, I did everything in my power to make part two of our fertility journey a success.

During part one, I had already learnt the lesson of surrendering and trusting the process. It was a lesson I hadn't forgotten. I had done my part. It was time to let the universe do the rest.

THE PERFECT CHRISTMAS GIFT

On 18 Dec 2023, we found out we were pregnant! I was over the moon but also quite anxious. Due to the fear of another miscarriage, I tried not to let myself get too excited or attached to the outcome, attempting to protect myself from future trauma.

My 8-week scan was scheduled for 10 January, and I wouldn't feel reassured until I saw my baby on the scan. I had been burnt before, and I didn't want to get my hopes up. The years of being poked and prodded, undergoing multiple surgeries and hormone stimulations, and experiencing multiple failures on the road to pregnancy were taking their toll. *What if this fails and I have to go through it all again?* We were onto our last embryo, so failure would mean starting the process over again, which would involve collecting more of my eggs. The process was physically taxing on the body, and a lot of my current fear came from the prospect of going through it all again. It had been a long journey, and I was tired.

But I knew the struggle was worth the reward. I wanted nothing more than to welcome bub number two into the world. We were so ready to invite more love into our lives and give Saige a little sister or brother. Deep down, I believed it would work, but I also allowed space to feel and process my emotions. In the lead-up to the scan, I decided to go easy on myself. Basically, I would wrap myself in cotton wool, love myself, and not let the fear and anxiety overwhelm me. I knew it was what bub wanted me to do.

WHEN OLD DEMONS RETURN

During my first pregnancy, the one that ended in miscarriage, I had a lot of anxiety, which manifested in vivid dreams. In those dreams, I could never fully see the baby's face, and I repeatedly saw myself dropping it on its head. It was distressing to say the least, and intuitively I think I knew that pregnancy wouldn't work out. While losing the baby was traumatic, it turned out to be one of those harsh lessons and blessings in disguise. If it weren't for the miscarriage, Kevin and I wouldn't have felt compelled to do additional work on ourselves, and we wouldn't be the people and parents we are today. When I fell pregnant with Saige, the feeling was different, and I wasn't haunted by those vivid dreams. I knew deep down that I was finally going to be a mum.

Saige is the most beautiful, placid child, and my life has been so blissful since she arrived Earthside. Interestingly, she reminds me of my dad. She looks a lot like him. We noticed it as soon as she was born. If I hadn't made peace with my dad and my past, it could have been a difficult situation. Perhaps subconsciously I wouldn't have been able to love Saige unconditionally. Maybe there would have been some resentment. I don't know for sure, but I'm thankful I didn't need to find out.

Although I tried to stay positive during my third pregnancy, I couldn't stop the fear and trauma from resurfacing. It felt similar to my first failed pregnancy, which only fuelled my anxiety further. Because I was in early pregnancy over the Christmas break, I didn't have work to distract me. Work had always been my outlet.

When my personal life got tough, I threw myself into the business. How many of us use work as a distraction? Whether healthy or not, it's a go-to strategy for many people.

Every time I went to the toilet, I checked the toilet paper, fearing any signs that something was wrong. Sometimes I'd have full-blown anxiety attacks. Even though I had done so much inner work in the lead-up to the embryo transfer, I still didn't have a good grip on my anxiety, and I wouldn't until I saw my baby alive and well on the first scan. For me, those first 8 weeks were hell on Earth. I couldn't stop thinking about the marathon ahead if I lost the baby again – all the procedures and needles. It was a real mindfuck. **The pressure for this attempt to succeed was immense, almost too much to handle.** Even though I had gone through the process several times and knew I could handle it, my thoughts and fears continued to get away from me. *I thought I'd dealt with all this...* Clearly, however, there was still a lesson I hadn't learnt, and the pregnancy revealed that I still had some demons to conquer. *I don't have it all figured out,* I thought, directing the thought at my unborn baby. *But I've come a long way, and I can get through this. We can get through this.* I needed to gain control of my thoughts, as I knew they could affect the outcome. Stress can be detrimental to a successful outcome.

In one breathwork session, I couldn't connect with my spirit baby. *Something's wrong.* However, towards the end of the session, I saw a white orb accompanied by a pink light and a strong message from my spirit baby. **"I've got you, Mum. It's okay to feel like this, but this isn't the first time you've felt this fear.**

It's okay to let the trauma go. Please get excited, because I am coming."

The following day, I felt much more hopeful. I chose to surrender to the outcome and trust that whatever happened was for the best. In the lead-up to the scan, I continued my breathwork each morning, along with journalling and angel cards. Over time, my anxiety faded into the background, and I was in a much more positive mindset. I had a blood test done at the Genea Hollywood fertility clinic in Perth, and they said my hormone levels were off the charts, which was a good sign.

A week later, I did an energy healing session with my healer, who helped me learn from my body and spirit that I didn't give myself the space to feel the grief from my miscarriage. I simply went straight into planning the next embryo transfer (Saige), which might explain why the fear was coming up now. My unborn bub wanted me to connect with her more, so I went back to doing the first trimester meditation I did when I was pregnant with Saige. The meditation, which I did twice a day, helped ground me in my body and prevented fear from taking over. Previously, the fear had been so overwhelming that I couldn't connect to my body or my unborn baby. I hadn't even noticed the pregnancy-induced nausea, which was a sign that everything was tracking well. When I was pregnant with Saige, I wasn't as fearful, as we still had one remaining embryo to fall back on. But I couldn't dwell on the potential for a negative outcome. Could I handle the worst-case scenario? Yes, because I had handled it before. I definitely didn't want to repeat the experience, but I knew I could get through it if necessary. The warrior within was alive and well.

Finally, scan day arrived. That morning, I was so anxious. My appointment was scheduled for 11 am. Just as I arrived, I received a text message asking me to come in at 11:30 instead. I didn't end up getting seen until 12 pm. I was already anxious, and the waiting just made it worse. The term 'scanxiety' is a common term used to describe the extreme anxiousness people feel in the lead-up to a potentially life-changing scan.

When I went in for my scan, I told the lady how nervous I was, so she worked quickly, putting the device on my tummy so I could see our bubba. When I saw the baby's strong heartbeat, I burst into tears. I hadn't even cried when I first saw Saige on the screen – I think I was shocked there was a baby there at all, as I was so worked up – but this time I couldn't hold back the emotion. It had been building up inside me for weeks, and now the floodgates were open. I felt so much relief. Suddenly, a huge weight had been lifted off me. Finally, I had confirmation that I wouldn't need to go through the IVF egg collection process again. I had confirmation that I would soon be a mum to two beautiful children. Our baby's due date was 21 August 2024.

 Scan the QR code to access the book bonuses and see live footage of these incredible moments.

FERTILITY FEARS CONTINUE

Despite my efforts in healing and processing my fertility-related trauma, the fear of losing the baby persisted. Every time I went to the bathroom, I braced myself for bad news.

I was caught in a cycle of guilt and negativity, chastising myself for feeling anxious about not being more positive about the pregnancy. If I felt like the baby wasn't moving, the fear would creep in. *What if something's wrong? What if something happens in labour? What if...? What if...? What if...?* Yeah, the what ifs weren't helpful, and I really had to fight to maintain control of my thoughts. Insomnia was a big factor in my anxiety. When I wasn't getting enough sleep, my thoughts would spiral more easily. Whenever I noticed myself going down that rabbit hole, I fought to pull myself back up. *There's nothing good down there, nothing useful. You'll only put unnecessary stress on you and bub.* I basically put myself on a strong leash, willing myself through the difficult times when they presented.

The first trimester was a war against anxiety, nausea, headaches, intense hormones, and severe pregnancy insomnia. Frequently, I'd wake up at 3 am, unable to get back to sleep. Knowing that sleep is important in early pregnancy made the situation even more frustrating. It was a frustration I had to overcome.

Combine it all with running a business and being a mum to an 18-month-old, and it was a gruelling pregnancy. However, as challenging as the insomnia and other pregnancy symptoms were, they served as reassurance that everything was fine.

The embryo transfer had been relatively easy on my body. It was my mental state that suffered. Because it had been so easy, I was on edge, thinking it would be taken from us just as quick. Throughout the pregnancy, I continued to struggle, which was okay. I'm only human, and the struggle is a part of the journey. This pregnancy felt so different from my pregnancy with Saige. I was convinced we were having a boy. However, in February 2023, we found out another girl was on the way, and my heart burst with excitement, not only for Kevin and me but for Saige to have a little bestie for life. I have two sisters, so I know how sacred the sisterly bond is.

A CATALYST FOR EVOLUTION AND SPIRITUAL GROWTH

When I was pregnant with Saige, I realised I hadn't really lost that first baby. She felt like the same soul. She knew we weren't ready the first time. She was teasing us, trying to learn how much we really wanted to be parents. As it turned out, we wanted it more than anything, and we proved it through all the self-development work we did to become the people our child needed.

Through spiritual guidance, I learnt that Willow will be my biggest fan in life. She'll champion me with all her heart. Our baby girl was grateful for all the work we did to both support ourselves and give her an amazing life. She was excited to meet us, and we were excited to meet her.

During my healing journey, I did some past life regression

therapy. Remember my ex who died in a motorbike accident in 2016? When we met, we had an incredible connection, but I couldn't explain why. He was like a twin flame from another lifetime, and after his passing I could still feel his energy around me. Generally, I'm in tune with people's energy, and I can usually read them without them ever opening their mouths. I sense energy in people and all around me, and I believe my ex was one of my spiritual guides. I could feel him with me.

Through the past life regression therapy, I grew to understand that he represented a fragment of myself I had lost when Dad left. Now that I had made peace with my dad, I no longer needed that missing piece. I was complete. Interestingly, after the therapy, I no longer felt my ex with me. I felt freer. I no longer needed his guidance.

My desire to be a mum wasn't just the catalyst for our fertility journey but also my spiritual journey. If I hadn't had such a tough time with fertility, I may not have gone down a spiritual path, and I wouldn't be the person I am today. I wouldn't have got to know myself on a deep level. I may not have learnt to love myself. I certainly wouldn't have developed the resilience I now have, an invaluable lifelong asset. As tough as it was, I'm incredibly grateful for our fertility journey. Looking back, I wouldn't change a thing.

Every time I've faced my fears, I've grown as a person, and my life has improved considerably. When I was considering leaving the first agency I worked at in Australia, I was up all night riddled with anxiety. I knew a confrontation was coming the next day. What would it look like? How would it go down? What was the worst-case scenario? Could I handle it? Yes, as long as I spoke my truth, I could handle the consequences. At worst, I'd piss some people off. I was practically already out the door, so I didn't have a lot to lose. When I did face my fears and stand up for myself, it was so satisfying.

Speaking your truth boosts your internal power and enhances your relationship with yourself, which only makes you fiercer moving forward.

> You realise you can call people out on their BS, and the more you do it, the less emotional it becomes. The anxiety that was so consuming the first time is barely a whisper in your ear because you now know the power of speaking your truth, and the warrior within is eager to rise to the occasion.

Facing the shadows of the soul can be scary, and many of us shy away from them because we're afraid of what we might learn. We don't think we're up to the challenge. We don't think we can handle the pain. However, refusing to face our demons causes more pain in the long term. They can grow bigger and nastier over time. They may even grow claws. The sooner you face the shadows of the soul, the sooner you can vanquish them and become the person you were meant to be.

Vanquish Senseless Fear and Anxiety

1. Don't be afraid to stand out. No one ever lived an exceptional life by falling in line and blending in with the crowd. Don't be afraid to take risks. Don't be afraid to question the rules. Don't be afraid to unleash your authentic self on the world.

2. Conquer fear by shining a light on it. When we avoid facing our fears, they gain more power over us. By identifying the root of your anxieties, you gain an understanding of them, realising that most, if not all, are baseless. The best way to fight darkness is with light.

3. Embrace failure. Don't let fear of failure hold you back. Each failure is a step forward, a lesson learnt. Every big success is made up of countless failures. When taking a big leap, ask yourself, *Could*

I handle the worst-case scenario? If yes, then you've got nothing to fear.

4. The ego is like an overprotective mother. Your ego will use fear to try to protect you. Sure, it may protect you from failure, but it will also bar you from success and growth. Don't let your ego keep you small.

5. Vulnerability is strength. Showing vulnerability isn't a weakness. Baring your soul takes strength, courage, and can have a transformative effect on you and those around you. We all have our struggles, so don't be afraid to admit when times are tough.

All love starts
with self-love.
Learn to love
yourself, and the
rest will flow
from there.

AWAKENING THE WARRIOR

10

KNOW THAT LOVE IS THE KEY TO EVERYTHING

ALL LOVE STARTS WITH SELF-LOVE

After my silent miscarriage in 2021, I realised I still had some inner demons to conquer, so I organised another intention-based psychedelic trip, this time using 5-MeO-DMT, also known as 'toad'. It's in tryptamine class and is one of the strongest psychedelics available. For the record, I'm not suggesting that anyone should do psychedelics. They're prohibited substances in many countries and, like many things, can be dangerous when misused. I'm simply sharing my own personal experiences.

After inhaling the DMT from a pipe, I felt the effects instantly. It wasn't like mushrooms, where there's a gradual onset and drawn-out trip. With DMT, the onset was instant, and the experience was short. As the effects took hold, I lay on the bed, and patterns appeared before my eyes. I then felt myself dissolve into the bed, and my spirit left my body. I saw everything that had happened in my life and all the puzzle pieces coming together. Then came the darkness.

In the darkness, I felt all the pain I had experienced in my life, but I also saw a brighter path forward. Before I could have the life I wanted, the child I wanted, I had to learn to love myself unconditionally. If I could do that, everything else would be okay. I also had to open my heart to love and the love of my husband. We both had our walls up, and I needed to let the love in.

I knew then that **love was the key to everything.**

Love is such a powerful force, capable of diluting every negative emotion – anger, resentment, bitterness, and hate.

When love washes over us and we truly embody the energy that comes with it, life starts to make sense. But you must learn to love yourself first, which for some of us, including me for so long, is easier said than done.

Through psychedelics, I was able to look beyond my own life and see the beauty and love in everything and everyone. We're born from love, and we're born to love. You're here in this life for one reason: to evolve with love and return to the essence of who you are. It's about coming home to *you*.

> Love is the currency of the world, the currency of the universe. It's the most valuable commodity we have – it has the power to positively shape our reality – but often we're too distracted to realise it.

Phones, social media, 24/7 news coverage – we're so bombarded with information and distractions that we ignore our inner selves. We forget to show ourselves the love we deserve. How can we learn to love others when we don't love ourselves? We can't. All love starts with self-love. Learn to love yourself, and the rest will flow from there.

INNER WORK LEADS TO LOVE

While psychedelics were part of my path to understanding the power of love, I know they're not for everyone. I certainly wouldn't recommend them to anyone, especially someone who hasn't done any other self-development, personal growth, deep reflection, and inner work with trained practitioners. Essentially, I don't consider psychedelics a starting point. You must be ready to confront everything that comes up during a psychedelic trip. The experience can be quite jarring and sometimes traumatic. For some people, psychedelics won't be a part of their journey at all. They're a useful tool, but not a necessity. There are plenty of other tools out there.

With the help of coaches and other experts you can work to peel back the layers, confront the darkest shadows of the soul, and learn to love yourself unconditionally. I chose the psychedelic route because I wanted to be a mum at all costs and I had nothing to lose and everything to gain. I had already done a serious amount of self-development by this point, but I wasn't quite where I needed to be. Could I have got there without psychedelics? Maybe. But after so many setbacks, I was willing to give any new solution a shot.

If my goal was simply to learn how to, for example, grow my business, I wouldn't have been ready to see what I saw. I wouldn't have had the courage or will to face all the demons that presented themselves to me. The flimsy goal of growing my business wouldn't have given me the strength I needed to work through the experience. I wouldn't have had a good enough reason to fight. If you're going to do psychedelics, your reason for doing so must be undeniable. It must be a reason greater than yourself.

When we began our fertility journey, I was naive about love. I thought, *When this child arrives, I'm going to give them all the love in the world. I'm going to give them everything.* As I did more inner work, both with psychedelics and without, I realised that the ability to give love wasn't the key. I also had to be capable of receiving it. Before my child could love me, I had to learn to love myself. If you can't love yourself, letting others love you is near-impossible. You can't understand their love for you when the self-love isn't there. It doesn't make sense. You owe it to your children to love yourself so you can accept their love too.

Kevin and I both had the same revelation. We needed to learn to love ourselves. We needed to become our own best friends. To get what you want in life, sometimes you need to fight. Often, however, you simply must learn to love.

BE YOUR OWN BEST FRIEND

When you've spent years being your own biggest critic, forming a solid friendship with yourself isn't easy. Yep, I know that particular struggle well.

As a teenager, my negative self-talk was horrendous. I was far from a friend to myself. Really, I was more than critical. I was borderline hostile. Not a great friend at all. If you're in a similar situation, still learning to show yourself a little self-love, be conscious of your mental dialogue and ask yourself, *Is that something I'd say to my best friend? If my best friend asked for my advice, would I tell them the same stuff that's running through my head?* Often, there's a huge difference between what we tell ourselves and what we'd say to a friend in a similar situation. If this is true for you, why are you telling yourself such horrible things? It doesn't help and will only ever hurt. I'm not saying you shouldn't be honest with yourself and own it when you mess up, but unfounded criticism, from yourself or anyone else, only damages your sense of self-worth. If it's not constructive, it's destructive.

Until I did the inner work and learnt to love myself, I kept falling on my arse. I didn't understand the full spectrum of love because I didn't receive what I thought I needed from my dad. As a result, I searched for love in all the wrong places, only ever finding more pain. However, once I shone a light on my past traumas, processed them, and accepted them, the shadows they cast on my soul evaporated, making way for love and compassion for myself and others. Finally, I was ready to not only give love but receive it too.

WILLOW HOPE RAYMOND

On 16 August 2024 at 2:07 pm, our beautiful miracle, Willow Hope Raymond, arrived 5 days before her due date. Her name carries a special meaning: Willow symbolises resilience and vitality. She immediately filled every crevice in my heart, and I was smitten with love.

Watching Saige embrace her role as a big sister was the sweetest experience. Her love and adoration for Willow was, and still is, truly heartwarming.

For the first 2 weeks postpartum, Willow was a dream – so peaceful and content. She loved her food, adored cuddles, and didn't have a care in the world.

A Very Different Experience

During my pregnancy with Willow, I was riddled with anxiety from residual trauma that had resurfaced. In true Sonja fashion, throughout my fertitlity journey, I used work as a vehicle to distract myself from feeling; healthy or not, that was my coping mechanism. I was balls to the wall working, speaking at conferences, trying to squeeze the most out of the time I had left before she arrived. I knew that once Willow was with us, she would need and deserve my full attention, and my time would be limited with a toddler and a newborn. Although I expected to be busy with a newborn bub, based on my postpartum experience with Saige, which I can only describe as calm and blissful, I expected another chilled child. Why wouldn't I? That was the normal experience, right? Right?! I soon received a harsh reality check. Initially, Willow *was* chilled – great! But it didn't last. Really, I should have seen it coming.

Towards the end of the pregnancy, I was in a lot of pain. In the final few weeks, I experienced a condition called pelvic girdle pain, and I could barely walk. Basically, pressure from my growing baby and softened ligaments due to hormones put extra stress on my pelvis, causing pain and inflammation.[14] For weeks, I couldn't socialise; I couldn't drop Saige at day care; I couldn't leave the house. I was forced to live like a hermit. The thing was, even though I wanted to be social, I didn't feel like being social. For me, it was an odd feeling.

When I consulted my healer, she explained that, during pregnancy, mothers embody the soul of the baby they're carrying. While I took it with a grain of salt, it did make me wonder if there was something to it. With Saige, I worked right up until I was 36 weeks pregnant. It was a chilled pregnancy, and she was a chilled baby. However, with Willow, I felt very inward-focused and less social, as if she were here for more than just a good time.

Because my pregnancy with Willow felt so different, especially towards the end, a lot of old anxieties around potentially losing her resurfaced. Two friends had recently lost their babies, one to a stillbirth on the day before a scheduled C-section and another to meconium aspiration – utterly heartbreaking. As much as I tried to stay strong, I struggled to push the thought of losing Willow from my mind.

I had originally been planning a VBAC (vaginal birth after caesarean). To help put my mind at ease, I saw my obstetricians regularly to check that there were no issues. Everything seemed fine; however, towards the end of the pregnancy, I learnt that Willow was measuring quite big, as Saige also had. This time, however, I had such a heavy feeling. I was constantly on edge, thinking I would lose the baby. My gut was telling me I needed to act – my anxiety through the roof. For years, I had surrendered to the experience of becoming a mother, constantly being poked and prodded like a lab rat, letting whatever happened happen, but now it was time to take back some control. It took me 2 weeks to decide, after so much back and forth and driving myself crazy about how best to have her safely in my arms. I finally opted for a planned caesar, scheduling Willow's birth for Friday 16 August 2024.

Honestly, I felt massive guilt for picking her birthday and messing up her astrology. I wanted her to come when she was ready, but in the end I had to accept that she could have come earlier if she wanted to and I was now doing what was best for her health and safety.

The C-section went great – she was out within 10 minutes. Amazing! Even so, lying on the operating bed, I cried the entire time. It was a very sterile, medical birth, not what I wanted at all. I wanted a water birth, but it wasn't meant to be. My fear of losing my baby was greater than the need to prove my womanhood by birthing naturally. All that mattered was that Willow was here, healthy and safe.

The Postpartum Struggle Gets Real

Like I said, the first 2 weeks postpartum were bliss, and I had no reason to suspect the situation would take a turn – and turn it did.

Suddenly, Willow wasn't peaceful anymore. She screamed and screamed and screamed all throughout the day and night. On a good night, I got maybe 4 hours of sleep. Most nights, much less. Her crying was hysterical and nonstop. I couldn't settle her, and I felt like a failure as a mum, constantly questioning myself. *Is she tired? Is she hungry? Is something else wrong?* No matter what I tried, she kept screaming. The only time she would relax was when I held her and my boob was in her mouth. Nothing else worked. As someone who's fiercely independent, not to mention ambitious, surrendering and slowing down were difficult. Willow demanded all of my time and attention, and I wasn't used to having the breaks slammed on so hard. During this time, there were so many tears and meltdowns (from me, not just Willow). The sleep deprivation certainly didn't help.

I felt a lot of guilt around the situation. *I know why this is happening*, I thought. *It's because I didn't allow myself to connect with Willow during my pregnancy.* I knew she wanted me to connect with her more, which was what I was doing now, but she had wanted it during the pregnancy. In the lead-up to her due date, I was so busy with work that I didn't allow myself the time and space to connect. Instead, I was running around on autopilot, often ignoring the fact that I was pregnant. Lesson learnt.

Searching for answers, we discovered when Willow was a few weeks old that she had collic, reflux, and also lip and bilateral tongue-ties, conditions that can cause a range of issues, including trouble feeding. Because her latch was so weak, my milk supply dropped, and I felt guilt about not being able to feed her. Willow underwent a procedure to correct her tongue-tie and quickly turned a corner, feeding like a champ and giving me the best gift I could have asked for – sleep! I also took her to a chiropractor, which helped tremendously, as she was a nightmare in the car. After 3 weeks of insanity, Willow was finally a much healthier, happier bub, and I was a much healthier, happier mum.

Once again, I was forced to surrender to the experience. I couldn't fight my way out of my current situation. Instead, I learnt to adapt to it. I needed to make room for Willow and her needs, even if that meant staying on maternity leave longer than I expected. With Saige, I was back at work a lot sooner. With Willow, I took the time we both needed, being present with her and enjoying our once-again-peaceful time together.

Through my postpartum experience with Willow, I learnt to be more realistic with my goals and expectations. I learnt to better adapt to changing and unexpected situations. I even pushed back the launch date of this book to focus solely on Willow and honour myself throughout the postpartum journey, knowing it would be best for us both.

THE DUALITY OF THE UNIVERSE

Just when I thought my postpartum path was beginning to smooth out, life threw me back into rough terrain. Life is duality, harmony, yin and yang. Without coldness, there can be no warmth. Without sadness, there can be no joy. Without death, there can be no life.

Three weeks after Willow's birth, I learnt that one of my best friends in Ireland was diagnosed with bowel cancer, and the prognosis wasn't great. For the weeks that followed, I was consumed with thoughts of losing one of my besties. At times, I was in denial that it was even real. I spent weeks crying multiple times a day.

Then on 30 October, I received a phone call from Ireland to say that my beautiful friend had lost her battle with cancer 2 hours prior. During one of the happiest moments of my life – bringing life into the world – I was forced to face one of the saddest – life leaving the world. The life of my best friend. Life and death pierced my heart all at once.

Even though she was from my home town in Ireland, I met her when I came to Australia. We became instant friends, soul sisters, inseparable for the year she was in the country, going to music festivals and laughing nonstop. We even got matching tattoos for our 30th birthdays, and she taught me to see the funny side of life. "YOLO" (you only live once) was one of her favourite sayings.

During my fertility journey, she was always there for me and was one of my main pillars of support. She constantly reminded me of my inner strength and resilience. Let me tell you – there were plenty of times when I needed that reminder.

When I learnt of my friend's diagnosis, it was a lot to process in such a short timeframe. Willow was already posing a challenge, and the heartbreaking news pushed me closer to the edge. My bestie was always on my mind, and I texted her constantly, sending her my love while at the same time praying for a miracle. With a warrior's heart, she vowed to fight fiercely no matter what. She fought valiantly, but her earthly fight was cut short.

Her passing caused me to question what truly matters in life. *Do I really want to continue to dedicate so much time and effort to my business? Aren't family and friends more important?* I delayed returning to work so I could focus on restoring myself. I was learning new steps to the dance of grief, and I hadn't yet mastered them. I still had some work to do.

To add to the catastrophic impact of my best friend's diagnosis, 2 weeks prior, my business mentor Kerwin Rae had suddenly passed away. I was forced to confront the realities of life and learn to accept the inevitability of death.

The life-death cycle is constant and unbreakable, and no matter how much we try to ignore or reject it, we can't escape it.

When I first met Kerwin in 2017, I had just begun dreaming of starting my own business, and I needed a mentor. At the time, I had no idea how much of an impact he would have on my life. His wisdom didn't just teach me how to grow a business; it also taught me how to become a better leader, how to stay grounded in humility, and how to push through challenges with resilience and heart. It was through his teachings that I learnt to lead with compassion, embrace uncertainty, and recognise that true success is about lifting others up along the way. I will forever carry his words with me, especially in moments of doubt, knowing that his wisdom continues to guide me, even in his absence. His legacy lives on in those he impacted throughout his life, myself gratefully among them.

Dealing with a double loss, the impact of grief was overwhelming. I was also struggling with Willow, which meant I couldn't just jump on a plane and fly to Ireland for my bestie's funeral, so I had to watch it via livestream, which was heartbreaking. I had made the trip especially back to Ireland in 2019 to be there for her wedding, but I was forced to forgo attending her funeral in person. Even so, I celebrated her in my own way, remembering her kind heart and how she lit up every room she entered, not just with her beauty but with a radiance that welcomed everyone into her world. I know she's now one of my spiritual guides, and I can hear her in my ear saying, **"You've got this, Sons. You've got this."**

There's not a single day that has gone by since her passing that my heart hasn't been utterly broken. She was my tower of strength during my darkest times, always lifting me up with her unwavering support. She radiated light, warmth, and love, leaving a void that can never be filled.

During times of grief, I've found that self-care is important. **Overcoming grief isn't a battle to be won with ferocity. Instead, it must be won with love – that is, love and care for oneself.**

To help lift the dark cloud of death that threatened to overshadow the joy of birth, I did all the things that feed my soul – beach trips, coastal walks, ice baths, saunas, massages – restoring myself so I could be there for my family. At a time when I could have poured energy into my business, I instead chose to pour it into myself. Gradually, my spark returned, and Kevin and I could enjoy the bliss of parenthood once more, but there will always remain a special place in my heart where my bestie is nestled forever.

KEVIN, A BORN FATHER

When Kevin and I crossed paths on the other side of the world from where we grew up, I realised he was everything I was looking for in a man: tall, dark, handsome, caring, and great with kids. I felt safe with him, which was important to me. Over time, he brought out the best in me, and finally my life started to make sense.

Kevin is the type of man most women would want as a father to their kids. Children gravitate towards him. He's incredibly in tune with them. It's his gift, which made the thought of us not being parents even more difficult to accept. Kevin was born to be a dad.

As it turned out, I was right about Kevin. He's the most amazing dad to Saige and Willow and an equally amazing husband. He's a real family man, cooking dinner every night and collecting Saige from day care while I work. He knows that, through my business, I'm building a future for our family, and he backs me 100 percent.

Saige and Willow have cracked Kevin's heart wide open, allowing him to experience a level of love he never knew existed. It didn't matter how we brought our babies into the world, as long as they got here. Seeing them all together, laughing and enjoying life, is so beautiful. I'm not the only one who thinks so, either. Although Willow is now only 16 weeks old as I write this, I've no doubt the bond between them will be equally as strong as what it is with him and Saige.

Once at a party, a woman approached us. She said to Kevin,

"I've been watching you, and I can tell you're the most amazing dad. See my ex-husband over there?" She pointed to a man sitting nearby. "He's fucking useless. You, on the other hand, are an outstanding dad." Hearing that melted my heart, and Kevin's too. He really is the best dad any kid could have hoped for.

ALL MASTERY IS SELF-MASTERY

In the lead-up to Willow's birth, I worked hard in my business to get to a point where I could accommodate another baby in my busy life. I wanted to live my definition of success, dance my own dance, which involves balance between being the mum of my business and a mum to my children. I didn't want to be torn between the two important roles. Instead, I aimed to create synergy, harmony, rhythm, because I knew it was what I needed to feel satisfied. With the right boundaries and strategies in place, I could be both a successful businesswoman *and* a great mum. Or so I hoped.

> It doesn't matter how successful you are in business, if you aren't successful in other areas of your life that are important to you, you won't be satisfied.

Think of all the billionaires in the world. They've reached the pinnacle of success in business, but they aren't always happy. In fact, some are miserable.[15] They have everything money can buy externally, but internally they're unfulfilled, and they may not even know why. If you don't define what success and happiness are to you, how can you work towards achieving? You can't.

So, ask yourself: *What does success look like to me? What does freedom look like? What do I need to be truly happy?* Whatever your ideal life looks like, the first step is to form a healthy relationship with yourself. You're going to need all the support you can get, especially from you, if you're going to achieve your dreams.

I'm not saying that wealth and material possessions can't enhance your life, but they shouldn't be used to fill a void. When I found out I was pregnant again, I bought a new car as my push present. I wanted something that would accommodate a bigger family, and I spent a good chunk of money to get the car I wanted. It was also partly a gift to myself for working so hard to make my business a success. I had considered getting a new car sooner, but I made a bargain with myself after a little mishap.

A year prior, I had an accident in my old Jeep. I rear-ended someone on the freeway in heavy stop-start traffic, so yeah... it was completely my fault, as I was seriously sleep-deprived and struggling with adrenal fatigue. After the accident, I decided I didn't deserve a new car until my driving improved. I had a lesson to learn and a problem to solve. *You need to learn to drive better, Sonja.* If I had gone ahead and got a new car then without improving my driving, I would have learnt the same lesson in a less forgiving way later down the track. Once my driving improved – no more accidents! – and everything else lined up, I was ready for a new car. Even though I could've just bought the car I wanted a year earlier, it felt better to earn it in different ways. It wasn't all about the money. It felt more in alignment with the universal lesson.

Although I'm sensible with my spending now, it hasn't always been that way. As I mentioned earlier, when I was at uni in Ireland, I switched from my Dunnes Stores deli role to a well-paying job with Meteor Mobile Communications. Great. The problem was, I'd blow all my wages on material objects – clothes, shoes, hair straighteners, whatever I thought would make me feel better about myself. During one particular week, I blew so much money shopping that I couldn't afford food, so I called Mum and begged for a handout. "I'm broke. Can I please have some money for food?" To my surprise, she refused – but wait, it's not as bad as it sounds. She did drive 2 hours from Tralee to Limerick to take me grocery shopping and stock my fridge with food, so I didn't go hungry. Looking back, it was the tough love I needed. Mums always know best, something you become more aware of when you become a mum. Mum knew that if she gave me the money, I would squander it, so she had to teach me a lesson.

Over time, I realised that money and material possessions don't equal true wealth. True wealth can only ever be internal, built upon a foundation of love for yourself and others. No external accomplishments can ever make us feel whole. The real work takes place on the inside, and all mastery is self-mastery.

A true warrior isn't just a master of combat and dance; she's also a master of her own mind. Once you learn to love yourself unconditionally and master your own mindset, your external environment becomes a much more hospitable place.

YOU'RE GREAT, BUT YOU'RE NOT GREAT AT EVERYTHING

While we're on the topic of self-love, which often leads to self-belief, I want to discuss the topic of knowing your limitations. *Limitations? What? Surely, I can achieve anything I put my mind to.* I mean, yes, as long as there are no completely impenetrable barriers between you and a goal, you *can* reach it. With hard work and dedication, you can be great at what you do, but you can't be great at everything. It's true for every human, living or dead.

For example, Albert Einstein was a brilliant physicist, but he probably wasn't great at basketball. Hey, I'm only assuming here. Similarly, Michael Jordan was one of the greatest basketballers of all time, but there's no way he could match someone like Einstein when it came to maths, although he did seem to break the laws of physics on several occasions. My point is, not only did Albert Einstein and Michael Jordan have different natural abilities, but they also spent their time learning different skills. They spent so much time and effort on their chosen practices that they became recognised masters. They were great at what they did, possibly the greatest, but they couldn't be great at everything. I'm telling you this so you know *you* don't have to be great at everything. It's okay to be humble and ask for help when you need it.

You're never going to be the smartest person in the room; if you are, then you're in the wrong room. Sure, you might know more about a certain topic than others, but they'll know more in other areas. When you start gaining momentum and success, it's easy to take the self-love a little too far, resulting in an overinflated ego. You're the bomb! You know it all! Nothing can stop you! While confidence is great, overconfidence is detrimental in the long run.

Staying humble gives you an open mind. You're more receptive to new information as it presents itself, which is crucial to growth. You can never know it all, and you should never stop learning. The key is to understand your strengths and weaknesses, and seek advice when necessary.

One year, I had five coaches. That's right. Five. It may sound like overkill, but I knew what I didn't know, and I knew I needed the help. And guess what? My business quadrupled that year. Why? Because I invested in people who knew better than me in certain areas. If I had let my ego convince me I was all that and didn't need the help, I wouldn't have got anything close to the same results.

In 2020, I decided to fulfil a lifelong dream and learn to play the decks. I was learning a totally new skill, and I wanted to be great, so I made a conscious decision to put in the effort. I could have half-assed it and kept it as a hidden hobby, but that's not my style. Instead, I practised and practised until I was good enough to DJ at parties, playing house music to crowds of partygoers and making them move. Know this – it's never too late to learn a new skill or follow a passion. But if you want to be great, you must commit fully to the learning process.

If you stop learning, you stop growing, and your business stops growing too. Loving yourself isn't just about building yourself up. It's also about being honest about your limitations. You don't need to be great at everything. You just need an open mind and a willingness to learn.

LOVE TRUMPS FEAR EVERY TIME

With every decision you make, ask yourself, *Am I coming from a place of love?* Too often, we make decisions based on fear and don't end up getting the outcomes we want. If, however, we make decisions solely based on love, we end up living lives that fulfil and energise us.

> **Replacing fear with love is one of the most powerful decisions you can make in life.**

Acting on fear can seem like the simple solution. In the short term, it takes less work and courage. But if you're only acting on fear, you're always running away from or avoiding something rather than moving towards your goals. With love and the courage to face your fears and fight those inner demons, you can have everything you want in life. It's a lesson that took me many years to learn but one I'm so glad I finally understand.

When we don't love ourselves, we're constantly battling inner turmoil, which makes accomplishing anything difficult. Been there.

> When we're at war with ourselves,
> we end up at war with the world.

Our perspective on everything is tarnished. If we can instead nurture and heal our relationship with ourselves, we gain a more favourable perspective of the world, which makes navigating it much easier. We see everything in a new light. We notice the beauty in every moment. Isn't that a much better way to live?

At times, we can get so caught up in our past and future that we fail to embrace who we are right now. The only moment that exists is this one right here, right now. You can't return to the past, and the future will arrive just fine without you dwelling on it. Is your mental dialogue speaking with love or fear? If it's the latter, it's time to tame the beast, whatever that looks like for you. **Learn the right lessons. Set the right boundaries. Make the right moves.** Until you tame the beast within and exercise some self-love, fear will dictate your actions, to the detriment of your happiness and wellbeing. Take control now. You'll thank yourself later.

I've known people who won't take the necessary steps to tame that inner beast. Fear rules their lives – fear of judgement, fear of failure, fear of vulnerability – and they struggle with their mental health for years on end. You can't help someone who's unwilling to face their fears and build a better relationship with themselves. Some people just aren't ready to face their own pain and trauma. Healing must start with you. You can't expect someone to suddenly appear with the magic fix. That doesn't mean others can't guide you on your journey, but you must be prepared to do the inner work yourself.

HOW TO START LOVING YOURSELF

Everyone's pathway to self-love will look different. By reading this book and reflecting via the included activities – you are doing the activities, right? – you've already taken a first critical step: you've educated yourself, examined your life, and shone a light on the shadows of your soul.

One key component to forming a loving relationship with yourself is doing things that light you up and help you stay grounded. Aside from the obvious – good diet, regular exercise, journalling, quality sleep, time with family and friends – I have one guilty pleasure, which I don't feel guilty about at all, that helps me recalibrate my brain after a big day of running a high-power business. Reality TV. While it may seem like junk food for the brain, to me it's self-care. It's good for my soul. I'm so proactive and busy in my own life that it feels therapeutic to sit back, relax, and observe others' lives for a change.

I'm also fortunate that my work is my passion. Few things light me up as much as seeing a business transform through the work I do. Having such a positive impact in the lives of others makes my heart sing. *Hallelujah!* The majority of the businesspeople I deal with are parents, and I know what it's like to grow up with parents who are busy trying to keep the family afloat or who are absent completely. Through my work, I'm able to help business owners work smarter so they don't have to work harder, which means they have more time to spend with their loved ones. I'm not just making a difference in people's businesses but in their personal lives too. Because I love my work and running my business, I feel fulfilled in all areas of life, living in love rather than fear.

MY LOVE AFFAIR WITH GOOGLE

Part of falling in love with my work was discovering the power of Google. I began my marketing career working in traditional advertising – TV, radio, print – that is, old-school advertising. Sure, the traditional methods still have a place in the modern world, but, in terms of return on investment, digital is king (or queen). Eventually, I discovered my true love: Google.

Years ago, getting ahead on Google was much easier. You didn't have to jump through half as many hoops to earn Google's trust. Nowadays, the fight to stay relevant is a ceaseless battle, which is why you can't let your SEO strategy grow stale. Just as the SEO landscape has evolved, and continues to do so, we must evolve with it, or risk extinction. It really is survival of the fittest.

As a small business owner, I know how easy it is to fall into the trap of wanting to do everything yourself, but for most people SEO shouldn't be one of those things. I've noticed a growing belief that anyone can successfully do SEO. The reality is, it's not true. Unless you're willing and able to invest endless time and energy into learning, strategising, and adapting, you're not going to have maximum impact. The skill set is so vast that to do well organically on Google via SEO, you need the following skills: SEO technician, web developer, SEO strategist, and copywriter. These skills are almost NEVER found in one person alone. In fact, you could find yourself sliding backwards or blacklisted by Google altogether if you make a wrong move. I've seen countless business owners learn this lesson the hard way.

One particular client, Rachel, comes to mind. After 3 years of us working together, she opted to start doing her SEO in house to redirect more of their budget to traditional marketing. Naturally, I advised against it, explaining how SEO could be delicate and that it required a continued expert focus, but she chose to go ahead with the change, which she thought was best for her business. Fair enough. As I watched from the sidelines, I saw their SEO go backwards and their website traffic plummet, ultimately costing them new clients and sales. Cutting their SEO budget had such a detrimental impact that they ended up coming back to The Search Republic after 13 months, with an increased rate to implement all the work that had been neglected over that period. Unless you're willing to invest the time and effort to keep your SEO up-to-scratch, you're better off hiring a professional when you can.

 To work with me for all your business needs, scan the QR code.

With that said, I've also seen people who have been burnt by putting their trust in a company that has taken a 'black hat' approach to SEO for quick results, leading to long-term pain when Google inevitably catches on and penalises them. When people get burnt, they lose faith in the idea that Google can work for them. But it still can *if* they're willing to approach SEO the right way. We have to be realistic with our expectations. Real lasting results require time and effort. There are no shortcuts.

Because so many people have got SEO wrong and failed, its importance has become diluted. Many people simply don't want to bother, and they look to social media instead. I'm not saying social media shouldn't be a part of your marketing strategy, but most platforms are incredibly noisy. Content, content, content, ad, ad, ad, look here, look there, content, content, content – *phew!* It's no wonder that getting noticed can be difficult.

When it comes to getting noticed, it's important to consider the mere-exposure effect, which is a psychological phenomenon where people develop a liking or disliking for things merely because they're familiar with them. The 'rule of seven', a widely accepted marketing principle, states that consumers need to be exposed to a brand at least seven times before they approach a business about their products or services. When solely relying on social media, gaining this level of exposure is difficult. This is because social media has become so noisy, which is why it's so important to adapt to the omnichannel approach to marketing. I have a seven-figure business with approximately 5,000 followers on the Sonja The Search Queen Instagram account, and almost

2,000 followers on The Search Republic, as I don't rely solely on social media. I use 17 marketing channels to grow my business. This is the main reason why The Growth Movement came about – to help business owners with their omnichannel approach to marketing.

 To learn more about The Growth Movement, scan the QR code below.

Now, more than ever, you need to fight to stand out in the crowd. What's unique about you and your brand? What problems do you solve? What sets you apart from the competition? It's not enough to simply say, "Buy my thing!" You need to earn people's attention and offer something of undeniable value. When I set up campaigns for my clients, I focus on the problems they solve for their audience. That's where the magic is.

On social media, people are constantly being hounded, and many of them are tired of it. *Buy this. Buy that. Look at my product. Here's a promotion. Look what I'm selling! Buy. Buy. Buy.* It's exhausting. You're selling something? Great, but no one gives a damn. They have no reason to care about the thing you're trying to sell. What do they care about? You got it. The problem you can solve. Put yourself into the shoes of your target customer. What can you do for them? What can you provide that will make their life easier? If you can identify and communicate the problem you solve, you'll stand out on Google and beyond, which is now more important than ever.

With so many businesses riding the digital wave, and rightly so, the market has become saturated. Even so, many business owners lack an understanding of what it takes to manage a successful campaign, and they often don't know what they don't know until they come to me and start seeing real results. When clients come to me, they never want to leave. Typically, the marketing quickly pays for itself as their profits rise, as long as they're willing to play by the rules, of course.

It is estimated that approximately 6.3 million Google searches take place every minute.[16] *Every minute.* Google is the most visited website in the world, so the potential for exposure if you can rank highly in results is huge.[17] Practically all of your potential customers are using Google, and, with the right strategy, you can leverage that fact. What's not to love?

Like I said, I love what I do, and I feel incredibly grateful to be able to do it every day. While I do help clients in other marketing areas, such as social media, Google is where my love lies. It's the backbone of what I do.

FORGET FEAR – ACT NOW

While I've achieved a lot in business and in life, my achievements aren't what make me happy, just as your achievements won't make you happy, at least not in the long run. It's not that

I haven't achieved enough; it's that accomplishments aren't the real key to happiness. **True happiness comes from evolving as a person.** I know it because I've lived it. Without the growth I experienced through struggle, I wouldn't be the person I am today, and I wouldn't be content, even if I had $1 billion in the bank.

Continual growth is key to continual happiness. We're all works in progress, and we never stop learning and growing. At least, we shouldn't if we want to continue to find meaning in our lives. When you're stagnant in your own life, you're not growing, and if you're not growing, you're dying. Growth is life. Growth is *living*. Would you rather be living or dying? I've experienced both states throughout my life, and I know which one I'd choose every time. I've lived in darkness, but now I grow towards the light.

> Don't let doubters, naysayers, the media,
> or even the government dictate your
> decisions and how you live your life.
> Too often, the influence of outside forces
> stops us from understanding what's possible.

We limit ourselves. We're overly self-critical. We dream too small. Life is short. A cliché, I know. But in relation to the universe, it's true. Taking chances in pursuit of your dreams is scary. But you don't want to act on fear, right? Ideally, you want every decision to come from a place of love. Besides, what's the worst that could happen? Don't go to your deathbed filled with regret. By then, it's too late to take action. The time to act is now.

INNER WARFARE: AN ACTIVITY TO AWAKEN YOUR WARRIOR

Live a Regret-Free Life

If you knew your time was coming to an end, what would you do? What sort of life would you want to have lived? What would you wish you had done? When someone has a near-death experience, it often changes their perspective on life. They value it more, and they're less afraid to take risks in pursuit of their goals. But you don't have to face death to start living. All you need to do is imagine how you would feel if death was calling. It may sound bleak to imagine your own impending demise, but it can actually be therapeutic.

For me, psychedelics were a useful tool for safely experiencing my own death. When a high dose of 5-MeO-DMT made it feel as if my spirit had left my body, I got to experience a simulated death, which involved letting go and accepting the situation, curing my fear of dying. It also brought to light the regrets I would have if I really were dying. The only thing stopping me from pursuing my goals, which included writing this book, was fear. When I thought about it, there were no tangible barriers. They were all in my head. Once I realised this, I was free to attack each goal with a warrior's heart, never again letting fear stand between me and what I wanted.

Ready to live a regret-free life? Imagine this is your last day on Earth. Think back over your life. Don't focus on what you did but on what you didn't do and wish you had. What important goals did you fail to pursue due to fear or other intangible factors? **Write them down.** Be as bold as you want. When it comes to your dreams, there are no limits.

What You Wish You Could Do

....

....

....

....

....

....

....

....

....

....

Now that you've made a list of the things you wish you could do, essentially describing the life you want to live, ask yourself, *Why aren't I already doing them? What's stopping me from making that life a reality? What do I need to do to overcome these barriers?* You don't need to live a life of regret. In fact, I strongly recommend against it.

If you're not living the life you want, you're not loving yourself. You're not giving yourself the love and respect you deserve. It's time to change that. **When you have a healthy relationship with yourself, the love radiates from you, and people and opportunities gravitate towards you**. You're in control of your own life; you're not following the herd, letting others dictate the direction in which you head. The more you carve your own path, the more you inspire others to do the same.

WORDS ARE IMMORTAL

Part of writing this book was wanting to leave a legacy. Long after I'm gone, my words will still be here for my children, my children's children, and their children to read. This book is my gift to them. I want to inspire them and let them know they can be and do anything they want in life.

> Ultimately, we're all here to grow, give, and leave our legacies in the world, giving future generations something to build upon and help them live better lives.

Think of all the words and inventions that have survived for decades and sometimes centuries. People still read the words of Socrates today and all the other great philosophers of the past. Benjamin Franklin's discovery of electricity changed the world in a big way, as have many amazing inventions. I'm not saying we can all be world-shaping philosophers or inventors, but we can leave something for those who come after us.

This book is my legacy. My hope is that future generations will read it, learn something, and draw inspiration from it. If my descendants want to know me, what I accomplished, and what I stood for, all of the answers are within the pages of this book. I want them to know what's possible, just as I want you to know what's possible in your life. I've filled these pages with truth and wisdom that will hopefully help others on their journeys. It's not the ultimate truth, and it's not complete wisdom, as I'm still a work in progress, but it certainly helps illuminate the path to a satisfying life.

> Once you can see the path, you must then have the courage to walk it. That courage comes from you. It comes from within. It's there – it always has been – but you must work to bring it to the surface.

Deep down, there is a warrior waiting to be unleashed. So, break the chains of past trauma. Vanquish unfounded fear and anxiety. Know that love is the key to everything. Only the present moment exists. How will you use it? Dwelling on the events of the past? Stressing about the future? Or embracing love and living life with all your heart?

Right now, I'm living a life beyond my wildest dreams. I've built a strong and healthy relationship with myself. I have the family I've always wanted. I get to do the work I love every single day. What more could I want? Of course, I'll never stop growing, stretching ever closer to the light, but at the same time I'm content with who and where I am right now. It is possible to appreciate the present moment while also seeking growth. In fact, it's the best way to live. While you can't ever fully master the dance of life – sorry, hard truth – you can become competent. You can become great. Importantly, you can enjoy the dance. Some steps, you will master; others will require constant refinement. The learning never stops. There's always room for improvement.

There's always room for growth. There are always opportunities to become more than you are.

Long after our bodies have returned to the Earth and our spirits have moved on from this place, our legacies remain, keeping us alive in the hearts and minds of those we left behind. The life you live now has the potential to create a ripple across time, impacting everyone it touches. The question is: What do you want that impact to be?

> The life you live now has the potential to create a ripple across time, impacting everyone it touches.
>
> The question is: What do you want that impact to be?

Know That Love Is the Key to Everything

1. All love starts with self-love. If you can't love yourself, you're not ready to receive the love of others. You're likely not ready to give love either. The strength of all your relationships depends on the strength of your relationship with yourself. Self-love is the foundation of everything.

2. Seek success in all areas of life. Being successful in business doesn't equal a happy life. Even the wealthy struggle with their mental health. Therefore, you should seek success in all areas of life that are important to you.

3. You can't be great at everything. While you can be great at some things, you can't be great at everything. Stay humble. Know that you don't have all the answers. Ask for help when you need it and be open to learning.

4. Focus on the problem you solve.
If you're running a business, focus on the problem you solve. Give people a reason to want your product or service. Success will flow from there.

5. Don't live a life of regret. What would you do if you could do anything? Well, what are you waiting for? Get out there and do it.

The search for
a wonderful life
ends here...

BONUS SECTION

COMING HOME TO SELF

Are you ready to take your business and life to the next level?

Join me at **sonjathesearchqueen.com** to take advantage of free resources.

If you're a business owner ready for more reach and visibility, partner with me and elevate your business to the next level.

Or alternatively, you can access **The Growth Movement**, my online program that helps small business owners scale to consistent multi-six-figure years. Utilising my most effective growth strategies, it's a fast track to financial freedom and living the life you've always dreamed of.

Connect with Sonja

To enjoy Sonja's **book bonuses**, scan here:

Need an accomplished keynote speaker for your next big event? I've got you covered. Get in touch via **sonjathesearchqueen.com**, and we'll make it an event to remember.

Let's connect! Follow me on Instagram **@sonjathesearchqueen** to join me on my journey and receive powerful tips and tricks to grow your business and enhance your life. Please know my DMs are always open.

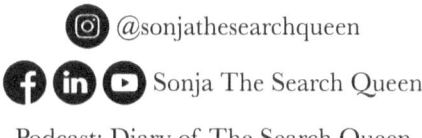

@sonjathesearchqueen

Sonja The Search Queen

Podcast: Diary of The Search Queen

Thanks for reading and taking this journey with me!

♀

All the answers that
we ever need are
within ourselves,
not within others.

ACKNOWLEDGEMENTS

Writing *The Search for Resilience* has been one of the most profound journeys of my life, and it wouldn't have been possible without the extraordinary people who have walked this path with me. This book is a testament to your love, wisdom, and unwavering support.

To my beautiful daughters, Saige and Willow: this book is my love letter to you, a testament to the journey your dad and I took to bring you into this world. It wasn't easy, but every step was worth it to hold you in my arms. My promise during those challenging days was to share this story so you'd know how deeply you were loved before you even arrived.

To my incredible husband, Kevin: thank you for your steadfast love and partnership. You have been my rock, my cheerleader, and my greatest source of strength. You've stood by me with unshakable belief and love, and I'm endlessly grateful to walk this path with you.

To my incredible mum, Joan, I am everything I am because of you. Your unwavering love, resilience, and determination have been my guiding light throughout my life. You've taught me what it means to be strong and to rise to every challenge with grace. From the sacrifices you made for us to the cherished memories, you gave me a childhood filled with love, laughter, and security. Your grit and devotion showed me that I could be anything I set my mind to, and for that, I am forever grateful. I am proud to be your daughter and a reflection of all your hard work and love.

To my sisters, Diana and Linda: Diana, your wisdom and

encouragement have been a constant source of strength and guidance in my life. You've always been there to uplift me, offering advice and support that I value deeply. Your steady presence reminds me of the importance of family and the unbreakable bond we share.

Linda, your joy and warmth light up every room and make our family brighter and better. Your humour and positivity have been a beacon during tough times, and your ability to bring laughter and love into every situation is a gift I cherish.

Both of you have been my rocks, my confidantes, and my forever best friends. I am humbled and overjoyed that Saige and Willow will get to experience the special sisterly bond that we share – a bond filled with love, support, and unshakable connection. Thank you for standing by me, believing in me, and always reminding me that I am never alone. I'm endlessly grateful for the memories we've shared and the unshakeable bond we'll always have.

To my incredible community and followers: your unwavering support, encouragement, and belief in my vision have meant the world to me. Every message, comment, and like has reminded me why I do what I do. You've inspired me to keep showing up and chasing my dreams, and for that, I will be forever grateful. This book is as much yours as it is mine.

To my team at The Search Republic: you are the backbone of my dreams. Your dedication, talent, and belief in our mission inspire me daily. Thank you for your hard work and for believing in what we're building together.

To the Dean Publishing team: thank you for bringing my book to life. Special thanks to Natalie Deane, editor-in-chief, for your extraordinary dedication in capturing its essence. Your love, guidance, and support have made this dream a reality, and I'm deeply grateful.

To all the incredible teachers and mentors who have guided me along the way: thank you for playing such pivotal roles in helping me overcome my deepest struggles, both in my personal and business life and for your support in helping me remove the spiritual blocks that once stood in the way of holding my precious girls in my arms. Mike Johnson, your dedication went far beyond a transactional relationship – you stepped in with unwavering support for Kevin and me during our toughest moments, and I'm so grateful to now call you a dear friend. Edwina Taylor, you guided us at the start of our fertility journey, helping me welcome Saige and Willow. Your support inspired resilience and self-growth, transforming my life. Ronán McKenna, your work as a breathwork facilitator helped me release deep-seated trauma. Sunita, your encouragement to leave my job and start my own business changed my life, and your guidance during our fertility journey means the world to me. Mitch and Mills from MJB Seminars, your teachings about balance and perspective have profoundly shaped how I view life's challenges. Joe Farkas from Pure Soul Wellness, thank you for your incredible work as a kinesiologist, helping me heal through trauma and neurofeedback. Adeel from The Modern Doctor, your commitment to supporting me during each delicate embryo transfer did not go unnoticed, and I am forever grateful. Aisha, your energy work has been a light in my life; you are a true Earth angel.

Veronica Pleij, your craniosacral therapy helped me relax into my body and release trauma. Courtney Wilder, your guidance in aligning my personal and business paths with astrology has helped me stay true to my purpose.

To Tony Robbins, thank you for guiding the way and for igniting a transformational moment in my life. Attending Unleash the Power Within in Sydney in 2019 was the catalyst for me to take my business seriously. Your work is truly profound and has left a lasting impact on how I approach my life and business.

To my friends and colleagues who took the time to read my book before it went to print, Laura Maher, Michael Daisley, Heidi Anderson, Mike Johnson, Laura Canham, and Tahryn Bolt: your willingness to carve out precious time from your busy schedules to support me in this labour of love has truly humbled me. Knowing that you invested your energy and care into my work has filled me with immense gratitude. Your feedback, encouragement, and belief in this project mean more to me than words can express. I am incredibly fortunate to have each of you in my world, and I thank you from the bottom of my heart.

To all of my inner circle friends: you know who you are. There are far too many of you to name, but please know I love you deeply and am incredibly grateful to have had you by my side on my journey of becoming a mum and a business owner. Thank you for always standing by me, even in my darkest days. Love you endlessly.

To Genea Hollywood Fertility Clinic Perth: thank you for the care, compassion, and expertise you showed throughout our IVF journey. You made us feel valued and supported every step of the way, and I am eternally grateful for the role you played in helping us bring Saige and Willow into the world.

To the talented photographers who have helped bring my journey to life through their incredible work: Zoe Claire from Alchemy Brand Studio, Anna Debenedictis from The Lifestyle Photographer, Mel Cieslik Photography, Michelle Boylan Little Wisp Photography, Kimmy Stevens Photography, Claire Day from Photos by Claire, and Steph White. Your creativity and vision have captured not only moments but also the essence of my story. Thank you for giving me memories that will last a lifetime.

My Granny Agnes: you were my number one fan, always cheering me on with love and pride. Your laughter, wit, and glamorous spirit brought endless joy to my life. You taught me resilience, kindness, and the value of family. Though you're no longer here, your love and lessons stay with me always, and you will always be my glamorous Granny.

To my Auntie Rita: you lived this lifetime with love and grace, leaving us in August 2023. You were like a second mum to me growing up, and I'm forever grateful for the love and guidance you showed me during the tough years of my childhood. Your impact on my life is something I will always carry with me.

To Alison, my peachy friend: losing you was one of the greatest sorrows of my life. Your warmth, laughter, and unwavering belief in me remain a guiding light. Your bold, loving spirit inspires me to live authentically and cherish every moment. Though you're no longer here, your presence is always felt, and your legacy lives on in my heart.

To everyone who has walked this journey with me – family, friends, mentors, and even the challenges – you have all contributed to my resilience and growth. Thank you for believing in me, guiding me, and reminding me of what's possible.

This book is for all of you, with endless gratitude and love.

TESTIMONIALS

Sonja's journey is a deeply moving testament to resilience, self-awareness, and transformation. Her story isn't just about surviving life's challenges – it's about facing them head-on, taking responsibility, and discovering the strength and answers that were always within her. What makes Sonja's journey so extraordinary is her willingness to do the hard work. She didn't look for quick fixes or external validation; instead, she leant into the process of self-discovery, knowing that true change starts from within. That mindset, paired with her unshakable courage, allowed her to not only rise above adversity but to transform it into something extraordinary.

We've been truly blessed to have Sonja as a client and to witness her incredible transformation firsthand. Watching her breakthrough moments – the ones that turned challenges into stepping stones – has been both humbling and inspiring. Her dedication, self-awareness, and willingness to say "yes" to every opportunity for growth have shaped her into the remarkable person she is today. This book is more than just a reflection of her journey; it's a gift to anyone searching for hope, resilience, or the courage to take responsibility for their own lives. Sonja's insights come from real-life experiences, making her words not only relatable but profoundly impactful. Her story is proof that even in the darkest moments, there is light – and with the right mindset, anything is possible.

It has been a privilege to work with Sonja and to witness her growth into the legend she is becoming. Her journey is a powerful reminder that transformation isn't just possible – it's within reach for all of us. This book is her legacy and a beacon of hope for anyone ready to embrace the power of actual transformation.

– Mitch J Behan and Emilia Tomei
Human Development Specialists

I've had the privilege of knowing Sonja for 5 years, during which I supported her physically and emotionally through her journey to motherhood, helping her conceive her beautiful daughters, Saige and Willow. Witnessing Sonja's transformation over these years has been nothing short of inspiring. From the early days of her fertility journey to watching her step into her leadership, build her business, and navigate life's challenges, Sonja has proven herself to be a true warrior. Even in the face of devastating blows and moments when her dream of becoming a mother seemed out of reach, Sonja never gave up. Instead of dwelling on the hardships, she looked within, found her strength, and kept moving forward. Her resilience and determination shine through every page of her story, making this book a testament to her unwavering spirit and an invaluable source of hope for others. As a fertility specialist and counsellor, my greatest hope is for all my clients to have the opportunity to become mothers. For Sonja, it was her persistence, hope, and unwavering commitment to self-growth that ultimately made her dream a reality. Through her dedication to clearing her mind, body and spirit for her girls to arrive, she not only welcomed her beautiful daughters into her life but also built a thriving empire, inspired countless women in business, shared her story on stage, and demonstrated the life-changing power of a resilient and focused mindset. I am so proud of Sonja and deeply grateful to have been part of her fertility journey

– **Edwina Taylor**
Fertility Specialist

I met Sonja nearly a decade ago where she'd attended an event I was speaking at. She came to me for a Soul Path Numerology Reading and I'd asked her straight away, "Why are you working for someone else? You need to start your own business." And her business journey began. Over the years, her business grew, as did her recognition as a dynamic and strong business woman. Exactly what I had predicted for her was in her soul path chart. We always stayed in touch and I thank Sonja for her trust in my guidance as a medium, mindset coach and numerologist. When Sonja approached me about her fertility challenges, I worked with her to address the energetic, emotional, and mental factors impacting her desire to become a mother. When Saige was born we also looked at Saige's soul path numerology chart as well, as the sessions had been so impactful for Sonja. It has been incredibly heartwarming to know that Sonja is proactive in her parenting. I have had the pleasure of watching Sonja grow as a business owner and a mother and am humbled that she is working to become more soul aligned to her greater purpose. Sonja has an incredible journey ahead of her and I look forward to seeing more predictions for her potentials materialise.

– Sunita
Medium, Mindset Coach, and Numerologist

When Sonja first came to us at the Modern Dr in 2021, her resilience and determination were undeniable. Despite facing miscarriages and major life challenges, her unwavering strength and commitment to becoming a mother were truly inspiring. Through a personalised approach focused on calming her nervous system and supporting fertility, Sonja successfully conceived and welcomed her first baby, experiencing a smooth and joyful delivery. In 2023, she returned with the same vibrant energy to grow her family once more. Together, we worked to create balance and calm, and once again, her dedication paid off as she welcomed her second baby. Sonja's journey is a testament to the power of resilience, love, and hope. It has been an honour to support her, and I'm certain her upcoming book will inspire countless others on their own paths to parenthood.

– Adeel Munshi
Traditional Chinese Medicine Doctor

To describe our dear Sonja, well I drew from something I heard about living a big life.

To live a big life, while some may assume it means to be big, loud and bold, in fact, means something deeper. It's to ask the big questions, to seek a deeper understanding and to discover our true essence, our authenticity and our autonomy. In doing so, we share our heart and soul with the world. Living a small life is to avoid those big questions, to just follow the crowd and to never look within. Ever since we met Sonja always asked the big questions. Still asks the big questions! Her persistence to dive deep into the depths of her being and to heal is brave and beautiful. In doing so, she has overcome a challenging fertility journey, bringing two precious beings into the world. Sharing her warmth, her heart and her journey is the natural process, and of course the result of choosing to ask those big questions.

– Joann Farkas
Counsellor, Kinesiologist, and
Neurofeedback Practitioner

She walks her talk.

I have known Sonja for a few years now, being her facilitator through breathwork and shamanism. Like a true warrior, she has faced her fears, not only conquering them but being the alchemist for her beautiful family and successful business.

She has worked with strong archetypes to transform and grow. I know how difficult it is to come from Ireland to Australia, the other side of the world, all family and comforts left behind, to embark on her very own 'hero's journey'. She's done it, and continues to help and inspire those around her.

Her resilience is to be honoured, and with her husband Kevin, they now have two beautiful daughters, Saige and Willow. She has shared her journey, the ups and the downs – so others can tap into the wisdom from these experiences. Seeking out the best, and even through uncomfortable times, has always shown up.

It's been an honour to work with Sonja,
I wish her continued success.
Go n-éirí a bóthar leat.

– Ronán McKenna
Breathwork Facilitator and Shaman

ENDNOTES

1 Bonanno, GA 2004, 'Loss, Trauma, and Human Resilience: Have, We Underestimated the Human Capacity to Thrive After Extremely Aversive Events?', *American Psychologist*, vol 59, no 1, pp 20–28, doi.org/10.1037/0003-066X.59.1.20.

2 Etymology World Online n.d., 'Warrior Etymology', viewed 11 November 2024, https://etymologyworld.com/item/.

3 Mingon, M & Sutton, J 2021, "Why Robots Can't Haka: Skilled Performance and Embodied Knowledge in the Māori Haka." *Synthese*, vol 199, pp 4337–4365, viewed 14 November 2024, doi.org/10.1007/s11229-020-02981-w.

4 Johnson, D, Policelli, J, Li, M, Dharamsi, A, Hu, Q, Sheridan, MA, McLaughlin, KA, & Wade, M 2021, 'Associations of Early-Life Threat and Deprivation with Executive Functioning in Childhood and Adolescence: A Systematic Review and Meta-analysis', *JAMA Pediatrics*, vol 175, no 11, doi.org/10.1001/jamapediatrics.2021.2511.

5 Tolle, E 2008, *A New Earth: Awakening to Your Life's Purpose*, Penguin.

6 Monash IVF, 'Infertility Statistics and Facts for Australian Couples', viewed 18 November, https://fertilitysolutions.com.au/infertility-statistics/.

7 Eunice Kennedy Shriver National Institute of Child Health and Human Development n.d., 'Infertility and Fertility', viewed 5 February 2025, https://www.nichd.nih.gov/health/topics/factsheets/infertility.

8 PR Newswire 2016, 'Visualizing Goals Influences Financial Health and Happiness, Study Finds', viewed 5 February 2025, https://www.prnewswire.com/news-releases/visualizing-goals-influences-financial-health-and-happiness-study-finds-300207028.html.

9 Ibid.

10 Arguinchona, JH & Tadi, P 2023, 'Neuroanatomy, Reticular Activating System', *StatPearls*, viewed 2 August 2024, https://www.ncbi.nlm.nih.gov/books/NBK549835/.

11 Caillet, A, Hirshberg, J, & Petti, S 2014, 'How Your State of Mind Affects Your Performance', *Harvard Business Review*, viewed 2 July 2024, https://hbr.org/2014/12/how-your-state-of-mind-affects-your-performance.

12 Firth, J, Gangwisch, JE, Borsini, A, Wootton, RE, & Mayer, EA 2020, 'Food and Mood: How Do Diet and Nutrition Affect Mental Wellbeing?', *BMJ*, vol 369, viewed 2 July 2024, doi.org/10.1136/bmj.m2382.

13 White, MP, Alcock, A, Grellier, J, Wheeler, BW, Hartig, T, Warber, SL, Bone,

A, Depledge, MH, & Fleming, LE 2019, 'Spending at Least 120 Minutes a Week in Nature Is Associated with Good Health and Wellbeing', *Scientific Reports*, vol 9, no 7730, doi.org/10.1038/s41598-019-44097-3.

14 The Women's 2019, 'Pregnancy-Related Pelvic Girdle Pain', *The Royal Women's Hospital*, viewed 30 September 2024, https://www.thewomens.org.au/images/uploads/fact-sheets/Pregnancy-related-pelvic-girdle-pain-210319.pdf.

15 Cockrell, C 2021, 'I'm a Therapist to the Super-Rich: They Are as Miserable as Succession Makes Out', *The Guardian*, viewed 23 July 2024, https://www.theguardian.com/commentisfree/2021/nov/22/therapist-super-rich-succession-billionaires.

16 Statista 2023, 'Media Usage in an Internet Minute as of December 2023', viewed 1 August 2024, https://www.statista.com/statistics/195140/.

17 Similar Web 2024, 'Top Websites Ranking', viewed 1 August 2024, https://www.similarweb.com/top-websites/.

AUDIOBOOK

Great news! *The Search For Resilience* is also available in audio format. Jump onto your favourite audiobook platform now and check it out.

www.ingramcontent.com/pod-product-compliance
Lightning Source LLC
Chambersburg PA
CBHW030253100526
44590CB00012B/386